# THE COSTA RICA ADVENTURE: A TRAVEL PREPARATION GUIDE

**SHONDA WILLIAMS**

All rights reserved. No part of this publication may be reproduced, distributed, or transmitted in any form or by any means, including photocopying, recording, or other electronic or mechanical methods, without the prior written permission of the publisher, except in the case of brief quotations embodied in critical reviews and certain other noncommercial uses permitted by copyright law.
Copyright © (SHONDA WILLIAMS) (2023).

All images in this book are from pexels.com

# Table of Contents

| | |
|---|---|
| **Introduction** | **9** |
| **Chapter 1 • Welcome to Costa Rica** | **13** |
| Brief History of Costa Rica | 13 |
| Why Visit Costa Rica? | 17 |
| **Chapter 2 • Planning Your Trip** | **21** |
| Best Time to Visit Costa Rica | 21 |
| Getting to and around Costa Rica | 24 |
| Currency and Money Matters | 28 |
| Accommodation Options | 32 |
| **Chapter 3 • Costa Rican Culture and Etiquette** | **35** |
| Costa Rican Language and Basic Phrases | 35 |
| Cultural Norms and Customs | 40 |
| Dining Etiquette | 45 |
| Dress Code and Fashion | 47 |
| Festivals and Celebrations | 49 |
| **Chapter 4 • Exploring Costa Rica's Neighbourhoods 53** | |
| The Central Valley | 53 |
| The Central Pacific Coast | 55 |
| The Guanacaste Province | 57 |
| The Nicoya Peninsula | 60 |
| The Northern Plains | 63 |
| The Southern Pacific Zone | 66 |
| The Caribbean Coast | 68 |
| The Isla del Coco | 71 |
| **Chapter 5 • Top Attractions** | **73** |

| | |
|---|---|
| Manuel Antonio National Park | 73 |
| Arenal Volcano | 76 |
| Monteverde Cloud Forest Biological Reserve | 78 |
| Tamarindo | 81 |
| Tortuguero National Park | 84 |
| La Fortuna Waterfall | 86 |
| Teatro Nacional Costa Rica | 89 |
| Rio Celeste | 91 |
| **Chapter 6 • Accommodation in Costa Rica** | **95** |
| Resort Recommendations | 95 |
| Hotel Recommendations | 97 |
| Villa Recommendations | 98 |
| Hostel Recommendations | 100 |
| Guesthouse Recommendations | 102 |
| **Chapter 7 • Costa Rican Cuisine and Food Experiences** | **105** |
| Introduction to Costa Rican Cuisine | 105 |
| Famous Costa Rican Dishes | 107 |
| Famous Costa Rican Drinks | 109 |
| Wine and Food Pairing | 112 |
| Must-Visit Costa Rican Restaurants | 114 |
| Culinary Experiences and Cooking Classes | 115 |
| **Chapter 8 • Outdoor Activities and Entertainment** | **119** |
| Canopy tours in Costa Rica | 119 |
| Coffee tours in Costa Rica | 121 |
| Surfing and windsurfing in Costa Rica | 124 |
| Volcano watching in Costa Rica | 126 |
| Nature cruise in Costa Rica | 129 |
| Watersports in Costa Rica | 131 |

    Beaches and Coastal Experiences    133
    Nature walk in Costa Rica    135
    Wellness: Spas, Retreats, and Yoga    137

**Chapter 9 • Shopping in Costa Rica**     **141**
    Fashion and Luxury Shopping    141
    Local Markets and Souvenirs    142
    Artisan Crafts and Workshops    144
    Antique and Vintage Shopping    146

**Chapter 10 • Practical Information**     **149**
    Health and Safety Tips    149
    Emergency Contacts    151
    Communication and Internet Access    153

**Chapter 11 • Recommended Itineraries**     **157**
    One Day in Costa Rica    157
    Three Days in Costa Rica    159
    Five Days in Costa Rica    161
    Seven Days in Costa Rica    163

**Chapter 12 • Travelling with Children**     **167**
    Child-Friendly Attractions    167
    Child-Friendly Accommodation    169

**Chapter 13 • Travelling on a Budget**     **173**
    Budget-Friendly Accommodation    173
    Cheap Eats and Local Food    174
    Free and Affordable Attractions    175
    Transportation Tips for Saving Money    178

**Chapter 14 • Day Trips and Excursions**     **183**
    Panama City    183
    Granada    185

Bocas del Toro 188
San Juan del Sur 190
Ometepe Island 192
**Chapter 15 • Sustainability and Responsible Travel 195**
Sustainable Tourism in Costa Rica 195
Eco-Friendly Accommodation and Transportation 197
Ethical Experiences and Wildlife Conservation 202
**Conclusion 205**

# Introduction

Costa Rica is a small country in Central America that offers a wealth of natural and cultural attractions for travelers of all kinds. Whether you are looking for adventure, relaxation, wildlife, or history, Costa Rica has something for you. In this travel guide, you will find everything you need to know to plan your perfect trip to this diverse and beautiful destination.

Costa Rica is bordered by Nicaragua to the north, Panama to the south, the Caribbean Sea to the east, and the Pacific Ocean to the west. It covers an area of about 51,100 square kilometers, which is slightly smaller than Lake Michigan. Despite its small size, Costa Rica boasts a remarkable variety of landscapes, climates, and ecosystems. You can explore tropical rainforests, cloud forests, volcanoes, mountains, beaches, coral reefs, and more. Costa Rica is also home to more than 5% of the world's biodiversity, with over 500,000 species of plants and animals, many of them endemic or endangered.

Costa Rica's population is about 5.2 million, with most people living in the Central Valley, where the capital city of San José is located. Costa Rica is a democratic republic with a stable and peaceful history, having abolished its army in 1948. Costa Rica is also known for its high quality of life, education, health care, and environmental protection. Costa Rica is one of the world's leaders in renewable energy, with more than 99% of its electricity coming from hydroelectric, geothermal, wind, and solar sources. Costa Rica is also a pioneer in ecotourism, with more than a quarter of its territory designated as national parks, wildlife reserves, and protected areas.

Costa Rica's official language is Spanish, but many people also speak English, especially in tourist areas. Costa Rica's official currency is the colón, but US dollars are widely accepted. Costa Rica's national flag is blue, white, and red, with a coat of arms in the center. Costa Rica's national anthem is called "Noble patria, tu hermosa bandera" (Noble homeland, your beautiful flag). Costa Rica's national flower is the orchid, and its national bird is the clay-colored thrush.

Costa Rica has a rich and diverse culture, influenced by its indigenous, European, African, and Asian heritage. Costa Rica's cuisine is based on rice, beans, corn, meat, vegetables, and fruits, with dishes such as gallo pinto, casado, arroz con pollo, and ceviche. Costa Rica's music is a blend of folk, classical, and popular genres, with instruments such as the marimba, the guitar, and the quijongo. Costa Rica's art is expressed in various forms, such as painting, sculpture, pottery, wood carving, and textiles. Costa Rica's literature is renowned for its poets, such as Rubén Darío, Jorge Debravo, and Eunice Odio.

Costa Rica has a lot to offer to travelers who want to experience its natural and cultural wonders. In this travel guide, you will find detailed information on the best places to visit, the best things to do, the best time to go, the best ways to get around, and the best tips and tricks to make your trip unforgettable. You will also find stunning photos, maps, and recommendations to help you plan your itinerary and budget. Whether you want to hike in the cloud forest, surf in the Pacific, zip-line in the jungle, relax in the hot springs, or learn about the history and culture of Costa Rica, this travel guide will help you discover the best of this amazing country.

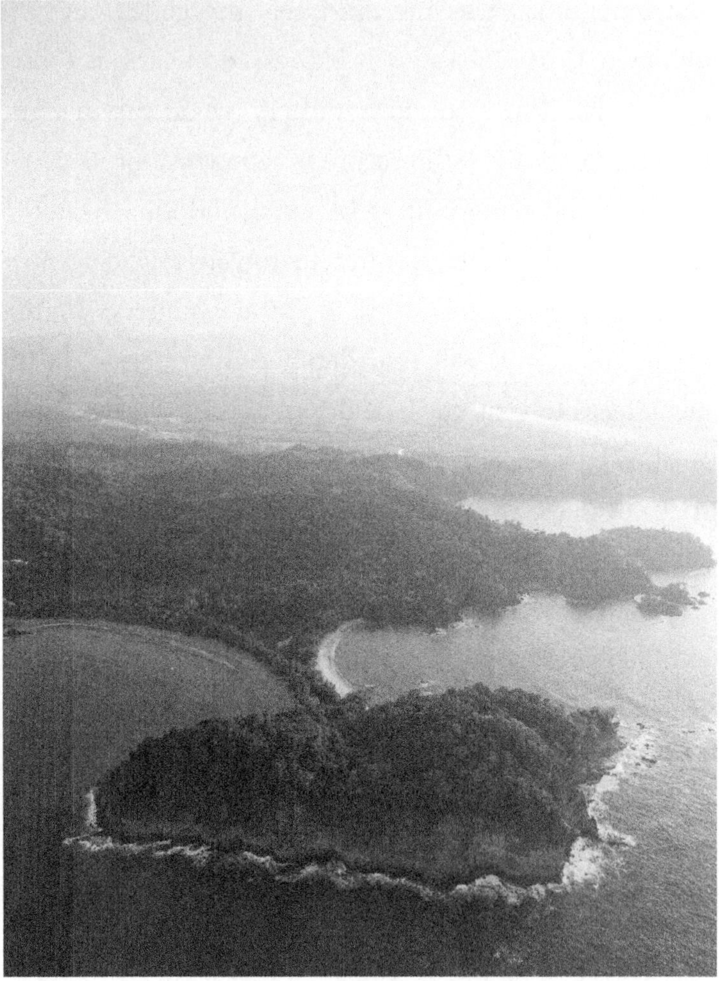

# Chapter 1 • Welcome to Costa Rica

## *Brief History of Costa Rica*

Costa Rica is a country with a long and fascinating history, dating back to the pre-Columbian era. Below is a brief overview of some of the key events and periods that shaped its culture, politics, and identity.

**Pre-Columbian Era**

Before the arrival of the Spanish, Costa Rica was inhabited by various indigenous groups, such as the Chorotega, the Huetar, the Cabecar, and the Bribri. These groups had different languages, customs, and social organizations, but they shared some common features, such as the use of stone tools, pottery, and agriculture. They also traded with other cultures in the region, such as the Maya, the Aztec, and the Inca. Some of the archaeological sites that preserve their legacy are Guayabo, Las Mercedes, and Rivas.

**Spanish Conquest and Colonization**

The first European to land in Costa Rica was Christopher Columbus, who arrived in 1502 on his fourth voyage. He named the area "Costa Rica", meaning "rich coast", because of the gold ornaments he saw on the natives. However, he did not establish any permanent settlement, and the region remained largely unexplored until the 1520s, when the Spanish conquistadors began their conquest. They encountered fierce resistance from the indigenous people, who fought to defend their lands and freedom. Many of them died from diseases, slavery, or warfare, and their population declined drastically.

The Spanish colonizers established the province of Costa Rica as part of the Captaincy General of Guatemala, which was itself a part of the Viceroyalty of New Spain. Costa Rica was a poor and isolated colony, with little economic or political importance. The colonists depended on agriculture, especially cacao, sugar, and tobacco, and later on coffee, which became the main export crop in the 19th century. The colonial society was divided into classes, based on race, wealth, and status. The majority of the population was composed of mestizos (mixed-race), mulattos (African and European), and blacks (African slaves or free).

**Independence and Republic**

Costa Rica gained its independence from Spain in 1821, along with the rest of Central America. It joined the

Federal Republic of Central America, a union of five states that aimed to create a unified and democratic nation. However, the federation soon dissolved due to internal conflicts and external threats. Costa Rica became a sovereign state in 1838, and adopted its first constitution in 1844. It also annexed the province of Guanacaste from Nicaragua in 1824-25, after a popular vote.

Costa Rica faced several challenges and crises in the 19th and early 20th centuries, such as civil wars, invasions, dictatorships, and economic downturns. Some of the most notable figures of this period were Juan Rafael Mora, who led the country against the US adventurer William Walker, who tried to take over Central America in 1856; Jose Maria Castro, who abolished slavery in 1824; and Ricardo Jimenez, who introduced social reforms and public education in 1914.

One of the most important events in Costa Rican history was the civil war of 1948, which erupted after a disputed presidential election. The war lasted for 44 days and resulted in the victory of the rebel forces led by Jose Figueres Ferrer, who became the leader of a provisional government. Figueres abolished the army, granted women and blacks the right to vote, nationalized the banks and the electricity company, and created the social security system. He also drafted a new constitution, which established the Second Republic of Costa Rica, a democratic and progressive state.

**Modern Era**

Since 1949, Costa Rica has enjoyed a stable and peaceful democracy, with regular and fair elections, respect for human rights, and a high level of social development. It has also maintained a neutral and non-aligned foreign policy, and has been a promoter of peace and cooperation in the region and the world. It has been involved in several international organizations, such as the United Nations, the Organization of American States, and the Central American Integration System.

Costa Rica has also developed a diversified and competitive economy, based on tourism, technology, agriculture, and services. It has been one of the pioneers of ecotourism, and has dedicated more than a quarter of its territory to national parks, wildlife reserves, and protected areas. It has also been a leader in renewable energy, and has achieved carbon neutrality in 2021.

Costa Rica is a country with a rich and diverse culture, influenced by its indigenous, European, African, and Asian heritage. It is known for its music, art, literature, cuisine, and sports, as well as its friendly and hospitable people. It is also a country with a strong sense of identity, pride, and patriotism, expressed in its national symbols, such as the flag, the anthem, the flower, and the bird.

Costa Rica is a country with a history of resilience, innovation, and vision, that has overcome many challenges and achieved many accomplishments. It is a country that offers a unique and inspiring example of democracy, development, and sustainability. It is a country that invites you to discover its natural and cultural wonders, and to share its values and dreams.

## *Why Visit Costa Rica?*

Below are some of the reasons why you should visit Costa Rica:

**Nature**: Costa Rica is a paradise for nature lovers, with more than a quarter of its territory dedicated to national parks, wildlife reserves, and protected areas. You can explore the stunning biodiversity of its tropical rainforests, cloud forests, volcanoes, mountains, beaches, and coral reefs. You can also encounter some of the most amazing animals in the world, such as sloths, monkeys, toucans, macaws, hummingbirds, turtles, dolphins, and whales. Costa Rica is also a leader in ecotourism, with many options for sustainable and responsible travel.

**Adventure**: Costa Rica is a destination for thrill-seekers, with a wide range of activities and sports to choose from. You can zip-line through the canopy, raft on the rapids, surf on the waves, hike on the trails, bike on the roads, kayak on the rivers, or dive in the ocean. You can also experience the adrenaline of flying over the Arenal Volcano, bungee jumping from the Monteverde Cloud Forest, or rappelling down the La Fortuna Waterfall.

**Relaxation**: Costa Rica is a place for relaxation, with a laid-back and friendly atmosphere. You can enjoy the sun and the sand on its beautiful beaches, or the shade and the breeze on its cozy hammocks. You can also pamper yourself with a massage, a yoga session, or a spa treatment. You can also soak in the natural hot springs, or sip a cup of coffee, tea, or chocolate, made from the finest local ingredients.

**Culture**: Costa Rica is a country with a rich and diverse culture, influenced by its indigenous, European, African, and Asian heritage. You can learn about its history, art, literature, and music, by visiting its museums, galleries, theaters, and festivals. You can also taste its delicious cuisine, based on rice, beans, corn, meat, vegetables, and fruits, with dishes such as gallo pinto, casado, arroz con pollo, and ceviche. You can also interact with its friendly and hospitable people, who will welcome you with a smile and a "pura vida" (pure life), the national motto and philosophy of Costa Rica.

20

# Chapter 2 • Planning Your Trip

## *Best Time to Visit Costa Rica*

Costa Rica has a tropical climate with two main seasons: dry and rainy. The dry season, also known as the high season, runs from December to April, and the rainy season, also known as the green season, runs from May to November. However, there are also regional variations and microclimates that affect the weather and activities in different parts of the country. Below are some factors to consider when choosing the best time to visit Costa Rica:

**Weather**: If you want to enjoy sunny days, warm temperatures, and less humidity, the dry season is the best time to visit Costa Rica, especially the Pacific coast and the Central Valley. However, the dry season also means higher prices, more crowds, and less greenery. The rainy season, on the other hand, offers cooler temperatures, lush landscapes, and lower rates, but also more rain, mud, and bugs. The rainy season is not necessarily a bad time to visit Costa Rica, as the rain usually falls in the afternoon or evening, leaving the mornings clear and sunny. You can also take advantage of the sunny breaks in September and October, when the Caribbean coast is dry and the rest of the country is wet. The rainy season is also a good time to see waterfalls, rivers, and wildlife, as well as to enjoy activities such as rafting, surfing, and fishing.

**Wildlife**: Costa Rica is a biodiversity hotspot, with over 500,000 species of plants and animals, many of them endemic or endangered. If you are interested in seeing wildlife, you can find it all year round in Costa Rica, but some seasons are better for certain species. For example, if you want to see sea turtles nesting, the best time is from July to October on the Caribbean coast, and from October to March on the Pacific coast. If you want to see whales and dolphins, the best time is from July to November on the Pacific coast, and from December to April on the Caribbean coast. If you want to see birds, the best time is from December to April, when the migratory species arrive and join the resident ones. If you want to see monkeys, sloths, frogs, and other rainforest animals, the best time is from May to November, when the forests are more alive and the animals are more active.

**Festivals and Events**: Costa Rica is a country with a

rich and diverse culture, influenced by its indigenous, European, African, and Asian heritage. There are many festivals and events that celebrate the country's history, traditions, music, art, and cuisine. Some of the most popular festivals and events are:

**Fiestas Palmares:** A two-week festival in January that features horse parades, carnivals, concerts, and bullfights in the town of Palmares.

**Envision Festival**: A four-day festival in February that combines music, art, yoga, spirituality, and sustainability in the beach town of Uvita.

**Semana Santa**: The Holy Week before Easter that commemorates the passion, death, and resurrection of Jesus Christ with religious processions, ceremonies, and festivities throughout the country.

**Fiesta de la Virgen del Mar**: A festival in July that honors the patron saint of sailors and fishermen with a boat parade, a mass, and a fair in the port town of Puntarenas.

**Día de la Anexión de Guanacaste**: A national holiday on July 25 that celebrates the annexation of the province of Guanacaste from Nicaragua in 1824 with folkloric dances, music, food, and rodeos.

**Limon Carnaval:** A 10-day carnival in October that

showcases the Afro-Caribbean culture of the province of Limon with parades, costumes, music, and dancing.

**Festival de la Luz**: A festival in December that marks the start of the Christmas season with a spectacular parade of floats, bands, and fireworks in the capital city of San Jose.

The best time to visit Costa Rica depends on what you want to see and do, and how flexible you are with your budget and schedule. There is no bad time to visit Costa Rica, as each season and region has its own charm and advantages. The most important thing is to plan ahead, do your research, and enjoy the pura vida (pure life) of this amazing country.

# *Getting to and around Costa Rica*

Below are some tips and information to help you plan your trip and make the most of your time in this beautiful country.

**Getting to Costa Rica**

The easiest and most common way to get to Costa Rica is by air. Costa Rica has two main international airports: **Juan Santamaría International Airport (SJO) in San José**, the capital city, and Daniel Oduber Quirós

International Airport (LIR) in Liberia, the gateway to the Guanacaste region. Both airports receive flights from major airlines and destinations in North America, Europe, and Latin America. You can find cheap flights to Costa Rica from various sources, such as Expedia, KAYAK, or Skyscanner.

Depending on your itinerary and budget, you can choose to fly to either airport, or even combine both. For example, if you want to visit the Central Valley, the Caribbean coast, or the south Pacific coast, you might want to fly to San José. If you want to visit the north Pacific coast, the Nicoya Peninsula, or the Rincon de la Vieja area, you might want to fly to Liberia. If you want to see both regions, you might want to fly to one airport and fly out from the other, or take a domestic flight between them.

Another way to get to Costa Rica is by land, from the neighboring countries of Nicaragua and Panama. There are several border crossings that you can use, depending on your route and destination. However, you should be aware that crossing the border by land can be a long and tedious process, involving paperwork, fees, inspections, and waiting times. You should also be careful with your belongings and documents, and avoid crossing at night or in remote areas.

**Getting around Costa Rica**

Once you are in Costa Rica, you have several options to get around the country, depending on your preferences, budget, and schedule. Below are some of the most common modes of transportation in Costa Rica:

**Private transfers**: This is a convenient and comfortable way to travel from one place to another, without having to worry about driving, navigating, or parking. You can book a private transfer service with a professional driver, who will pick you up and drop you off at your desired locations, and also assist you with your luggage and any requests you might have. You can find reliable and affordable private transfer services from various providers, such as Erick Tours Costa Rica Transportation or Transportation in Costa Rica.

**Shared shuttles**: This is a cheaper and more social way to travel between the main tourist destinations in Costa Rica, sharing a van or a bus with other travelers. You can book a shared shuttle service with a reputable company, who will arrange the pickup and drop-off times and locations, and also provide you with a safe and comfortable ride. You can find various options and prices for shared shuttles.

**Public buses**: This is the cheapest and most authentic way to travel around Costa Rica, using the same means of transportation as the locals. You can find public buses that connect almost every town and city in the country, with different schedules and frequencies. However, you should be prepared for some inconveniences, such as delays, crowds, noise, and lack of comfort. You should also be careful with your belongings and documents, and avoid traveling at night or in unfamiliar areas.

**Rental cars**: This is a flexible and adventurous way to travel around Costa Rica, giving you the freedom and independence to explore the country at your own pace and style. You can rent a car from various agencies and locations in the country, choosing the type and size of vehicle that suits your needs and budget. However, you should be aware that driving in Costa Rica can be challenging, due to the road conditions, traffic, signage, and regulations. You should also consider the costs and risks of renting a car, such as insurance, gas, tolls, parking, and fines.

**Domestic flights**: This is a fast and convenient way to travel between the main regions and attractions in Costa Rica, saving you time and hassle. You can book a domestic flight with one of the local airlines, such as

Sansa or Skyway, who operate small planes that fly to various destinations in the country. However, you should be aware that flying in Costa Rica can be expensive, limited, and unpredictable, depending on the availability, demand, and weather. You should also consider the restrictions and regulations of flying, such as baggage, check-in, and security.

As you can see, getting to and around Costa Rica can be a fun and rewarding experience, if you plan ahead and choose the best option for your trip. No matter how you travel, you will be amazed by the beauty and diversity of this country, and the hospitality and kindness of its people.

## *Currency and Money Matters*

Costa Rica uses two currencies: the Costa Rican colón (CRC) and the US dollar (USD). The colón is the official currency, but the dollar is widely accepted and sometimes preferred. In this section, you will learn about the currency and money matters in Costa Rica, such as how to exchange money, how to use credit cards and ATMs, and how to tip and bargain.

**The Costa Rican colón**

The Costa Rican colón is named after Christopher

Columbus, who visited the country in 1502. The colón is divided into 100 centimos, and has colorful bills and coins that feature the country's wildlife and culture. The bills come in denominations of 1,000, 2,000, 5,000, 10,000, 20,000, and 50,000 colones, and the coins come in denominations of 5, 10, 25, 50, 100, and 500 colones. The exchange rate between the colón and the dollar fluctuates daily.

**The US dollar**

The US dollar is also widely used and accepted in Costa Rica, especially in tourist areas and businesses. However, you should always carry some colones with you, as some places may not accept dollars, or may give you a less favorable exchange rate. You should also bring smaller bills, such as $1, $5, $10, and $20, as larger bills may be harder to change or may raise suspicion of counterfeiting. You should also avoid bills that are torn, stained, or damaged, as they may be rejected.

**Exchanging money**

You can exchange money for Costa Rican currency at any local bank, some hotels, or authorized exchange offices. However, you should avoid exchanging money at the airport, as they usually offer the worst rates. You should also avoid exchanging money on the street, as it may be illegal or unsafe. You can also exchange money at your own bank in your home country, but you may need to order the colones in advance and pay a higher fee.

**Using credit cards and ATMs**

Credit cards are widely accepted in Costa Rica, especially Visa and MasterCard. You can use them to pay for hotels, restaurants, tours, and other services. However, you should always check the exchange rate and the fees that your card issuer may charge for foreign transactions. You should also notify your bank before traveling to Costa Rica, to avoid any problems or fraud alerts. You should also keep your receipts and check your statements regularly.

ATMs are also widely available in Costa Rica, and you can use them to withdraw colones or dollars from your debit or credit card. However, you should also check the fees and limits that your bank may charge for using an ATM abroad. You should also look for ATMs that belong to reputable banks or networks, and avoid using them at night or in isolated areas. You should also protect your PIN and card from skimming or theft.

**Tipping and bargaining**

Tipping is customary in Costa Rica, but not mandatory.

You can tip according to the quality of the service and your satisfaction. Below are some general guidelines for tipping in Costa Rica:

**Restaurants and bars**: Most restaurants and bars include a 10% service charge and a 13% sales tax in the bill. You can leave an additional tip of 5-10% if you are happy with the service, or none if you are not. You can tip in colones or dollars, but preferably in cash.

**Hotels**: You can tip the bellboys, maids, and concierges according to the level and duration of their service. A common amount is $1-2 per bag, per day, or per request. You can tip in colones or dollars, but preferably in cash.

**Tours and activities**: You can tip the guides, drivers, and instructors according to the quality and length of the tour or activity. A common amount is $5-10 per person, per day, or per activity. You can tip in colones or dollars, but preferably in cash.

**Taxis**: Tipping is not expected for taxis, as they use a meter or a fixed rate. However, you can round up the fare or leave a small tip if you are satisfied with the service or if the driver helps you with your luggage. You can tip in colones or dollars, but preferably in cash.

Bargaining is not very common in Costa Rica, except in some markets or souvenir shops. You can try to negotiate a lower price, but always politely and respectfully. You should also have a realistic expectation of how much you can save, and be prepared to walk away if you are not happy with the offer. You should also pay in colones, as paying in dollars may increase the price.

## *Accommodation Options*

Below are some of the types of properties that you can stay in Costa Rica:

**Hotels and resorts**: These are typically luxurious and comfortable accommodations with a range of nice amenities like spas, restaurants, and pools. You can find hotels and resorts in various locations, such as the city, the beach, or the mountains. Some of the best hotels and resorts in Costa Rica are Sheraton San Jose Hotel, Dreams Las Mareas All Inclusive, and Four Seasons Resort Costa Rica at Peninsula Papagayo.

**Vacation homes**: These are popular options for families and groups traveling together, as they offer more space, privacy, and flexibility. You can book vacation homes that often come with a full kitchen, outdoor space, and other facilities. You can find vacation homes in different settings, such as the rainforest, the countryside, or the coast. Some of the best vacation homes in Costa Rica are Casa Chameleon at Mal Pais, Casa Oceano, and Villa Manzu.

**Villas**: These are often large and luxurious properties that offer complete privacy and space. You can rent villas that have multiple bedrooms, bathrooms, living areas, and amenities. You can find villas in stunning locations, such as the hilltop, the beachfront, or the island. Some of the best villas in Costa Rica are Villa Punto de Vista, Villa Estrella, and Villa Paraiso.

**Hostels**: These are cheap and cheerful accommodations that cater to backpackers, solo travelers, and young people. You can stay in hostels that offer dorms, private rooms, or shared facilities. You can find hostels in lively areas, such as the city center, the surf town, or the national park. Some of the best hostels in Costa Rica are Selina San Jose, Selina La Fortuna, and Selina Manuel Antonio.

**Eco-lodges**: These are environmentally friendly and sustainable accommodations that blend with nature and support local communities. You can stay in eco-lodges that offer rustic cabins, tents, or treehouses. You can find eco-lodges in remote and wild areas, such as the jungle, the volcano, or the mangrove. Some of the best eco-lodges in Costa Rica are Lapa Rios Lodge, Pacuare Lodge, and Finca Bellavista.

# Chapter 3 • Costa Rican Culture and Etiquette

## *Costa Rican Language and Basic Phrases*

Costa Rica is a Spanish-speaking country, but it has its own dialect, accent, and slang that make it unique and distinctive. If you want to communicate with the locals, learn about their culture, and have a more enjoyable and authentic experience, you should learn some of the basic phrases and expressions of Costa Rican Spanish. Below are some of the things you should know about the language and some of the most useful and common phrases you can use in Costa Rica.

**The Language**

Costa Rican Spanish is a variant of Central American Spanish, which is influenced by the indigenous, European, African, and Asian heritage of the region. Costa Rican Spanish has some features that distinguish it from other Spanish dialects, such as:

The use of the second-person singular pronoun vos instead of tú to address someone informally. Vos is conjugated differently from tú, for example: vos sos (you are), vos tenés (you have), vos querés (you want).

The use of the suffix -ico or -ica to form diminutives, instead of -ito or -ita. For example: chiquitico (very small), cafecito (little coffee), momentico (little moment).

The use of the interjection diay to express surprise, doubt, or curiosity. For example: Diay, ¿qué pasó? (What happened?), Diay, ¿y eso? (And that?), Diay, ¿cómo está? (How are you?).

The use of the word mae to refer to a friend, a dude, or a person in general. Mae is equivalent to the Mexican güey or the Argentine che. For example: ¿Qué hacés, mae? (What are you doing, dude?), Mae, eso está tuanis (Dude, that's cool), Mae, no seás así (Dude, don't be like that).

The use of the word tuanis to express something cool, good, or nice. Tuanis is derived from the English word "too nice". For example: La playa está tuanis (The beach is cool), El concierto estuvo tuanis (The concert was good), Gracias, tuanis (Thanks, nice).

**The Phrases**

Below are some of the most common and useful phrases and words that you can use in Costa Rica, organized by category:

**Greetings and Farewells**

Hola (Hello)

Buenos días (Good morning)

Buenas tardes (Good afternoon)

Buenas noches (Good evening/night)

Cómo está? (How are you? - formal)

Cómo estás? (How are you? - informal)

Qué tal? (How is it going?)

Bien, gracias (Fine, thank you)

Y vos? (And you? - informal)

Y usted? (And you? - formal)

Mucho gusto (Nice to meet you)

Encantado/a (Pleased to meet you)

Adiós (Goodbye)

Hasta luego (See you later)

Hasta pronto (See you soon)

Chao (Bye)

Pura vida (Pure life - a typical Costa Rican expression that can mean hello, goodbye, thank you, you're welcome, or anything positive)

Courtesy and Politeness

Por favor (Please)

Gracias (Thank you)

De nada (You're welcome)

Con permiso (Excuse me - to get by someone)

Disculpe (Excuse me - to get someone's attention)

Perdón (Sorry - to apologize or to ask someone to repeat something)

Lo siento (I'm sorry - to express regret or sympathy)

Salud (Bless you - after someone sneezes)

Salud (Cheers - when toasting)

Buen provecho (Enjoy your meal)

Igualmente (Likewise - to return a compliment or a wish)

**Questions and Answers**

Qué? (What?)

Quién? (Who?)

Cuándo? (When?)

Dónde? (Where?)

Cómo? (How?)

Por qué? (Why?)

Para qué? (What for?)

Cuánto/a? (How much?)

Cuántos/as? (How many?)

Qué hora es? (What time is it?)

Qué día es hoy? (What day is today?)

Qué fecha es hoy? (What date is today?)

Cómo se dice ... en español? (How do you say ... in Spanish?)

Dónde está el aeropuerto? (Where is the airport?)

Dónde está el hotel? (Where is the hotel?)

Dónde está el restaurante? (Where is the restaurant?)

Dónde está el banco? (Where is the bank?)

Dónde está el supermercado? (Where is the supermarket?)

Dónde está la farmacia? (Where is the pharmacy?)

Dónde está la estación de autobuses? (Where is the bus station?)

Dónde está la estación de trenes? (Where is the train station?)

Dónde está la parada de taxis? (Where is the taxi stand?)

Dónde está el museo? (Where is the museum?)

Dónde está el parque? (Where is the park?)

Dónde está la playa? (Where is the beach?)

Dónde está la iglesia? (Where is the church?)

Dónde está el hospital? (Where is the hospital?)

Dónde está el correo? (Where is the post office?)

To answer these questions, you can use the following expressions:

Está ... (It is ...)

Está cerca de ... (It is near ...)

Está lejos de ... (It is far from ...)

Está al lado de ... (It is next to ...)

Está enfrente de ... (It is in front of ...)

Está detrás de ... (It is behind ...)

Está a la derecha de ... (It is to the right of ...)

Está a la izquierda de ... (It is to the left of ...)

Está arriba de ... (It is above ...)

Está abajo de ... (It is below ...)

Está entre ... y ... (It is between ... and ...)

Está en la esquina de ... y ... (It is on the corner of ... and ...)

Está en la calle ... (It is on the street ...)

Está en la avenida ... (It is on the avenue ...)

Está en el centro de ... (It is in the center of ...)

For example, if you want to ask where the airport is, you can say:

Dónde está el aeropuerto? (Where is the airport?)

And if you want to answer that the airport is far from the city, you can say:

Está lejos de la ciudad. (It is far from the city.)

## *Cultural Norms and Customs*

Costa Rica is a country with a rich and diverse culture, influenced by its indigenous, European, African, and

Asian heritage. Costa Ricans, or Ticos as they are affectionately called, are known for their friendliness, hospitality, and happiness. However, they also have their own norms and customs that may differ from those of other countries. If you want to have a smooth and respectful interaction with the locals, you should learn some of the basic aspects of Costa Rican culture, such as:

**Greetings and Farewells**

Costa Ricans are very warm and polite when greeting each other, and they usually use a light kiss on the cheek, a handshake, or a hug, depending on the level of familiarity and formality. They also use various expressions to say hello, such as "Buenos días" (Good morning), "Buenas tardes" (Good afternoon), or "Pura vida" (Pure life), which is a typical Costa Rican phrase that can mean anything positive. When addressing someone, they use the second-person singular pronoun "vos" instead of "tú" to show informality and closeness, and they use the honorific titles "don" and "doña" before the first name to show respect and courtesy. When saying goodbye, they may use the same expressions as for greeting, or simply say "Adiós" (Goodbye), "Hasta luego" (See you later), "Hasta pronto" (See you soon), or "Chao" (Bye).

**Family Values**

Family is very important in Costa Rica, and it often includes extended relatives who live nearby or visit frequently. Costa Ricans are very protective and supportive of their family members, and they expect visitors to show interest and appreciation for their family as well. Family gatherings are common and festive, especially during holidays and celebrations, such as Christmas, New Year, Easter, and birthdays. Costa Ricans also value children and treat them with affection and indulgence, sometimes calling them "rey" or "reina" (king or queen).

**Religion**

Costa Rica is a predominantly Roman Catholic country, and religion plays a significant role in its culture and society. Costa Ricans attend mass regularly, celebrate religious holidays and festivals, and display religious symbols and images in their homes and public places. Some of the most important religious events are Semana Santa (Holy Week), which commemorates the passion, death, and resurrection of Jesus Christ; Fiesta de la Virgen de los Ángeles (Feast of the Virgin of the Angels), which honors the patron saint of Costa Rica; and Día de los Muertos (Day of the Dead), which remembers the deceased loved ones.

**Etiquette**

Costa Ricans are very well-mannered and expect visitors to behave accordingly. Some of the basic rules of etiquette are:

Be punctual for formal or business appointments, but be flexible for social or casual occasions, as Costa Ricans may not be very strict with time.

Dress appropriately for the occasion, avoiding revealing or sloppy clothing, especially in religious or official settings.

Use polite and respectful language, avoiding profanity, slang, or jokes that may offend or embarrass others.

Avoid topics that may cause controversy or conflict, such as politics, religion, or personal issues, and respect the opinions and beliefs of others.

Accept invitations and offers with gratitude and enthusiasm, and reciprocate them if possible.

Bring a small gift, such as flowers, chocolates, or wine, when visiting someone's home, and compliment the host on their hospitality and food.

Eat with a knife and fork, and keep your hands above the table, unless you are eating finger food or a typical dish, such as gallo pinto (rice and beans).

Tip 10% of the bill in restaurants and bars, unless the service charge is already included, and tip other service providers, such as taxi drivers, hotel staff, or tour guides, according to your satisfaction.

**Slang**

Costa Ricans have their own dialect and slang that make their Spanish unique and distinctive. Some of the most common and useful words and phrases that you can use in Costa Rica are:

**Mae**: A word that means dude, friend, or person, and can be used to address anyone informally. For example: "¿Qué hacés, mae?" (What are you doing, dude?).

**Tuanis**: A word that means cool, good, or nice, and can be used to describe anything positive. For example: "La playa está tuanis" (The beach is cool).

**Diay**: An interjection that expresses surprise, doubt, or curiosity, and can be used to start or end a question. For example: "Diay, ¿qué pasó?" (What happened?).

**Pura vida**: A phrase that means pure life, and can be used to say hello, goodbye, thank you, you're welcome, or anything positive. For example: "Pura vida, mae" (Pure life, dude).

**Upe**: A word that means hello, and can be used to announce your arrival or presence at someone's door or place. For example: "Upe, ¿hay alguien?" (Hello, is anyone there?).

## *Dining Etiquette*

Below are some of the tips and information that you should know about dining etiquette in Costa Rica:

When you are invited to a meal at someone's home, you should arrive on time or slightly late, but not too early. You should also bring a small gift, such as flowers, chocolates, or wine, and compliment the host on their hospitality and food. You should not start eating until the host says "Buen provecho" (Enjoy your meal), and you should finish everything on your plate, unless you are offered more, in which case you can politely decline. You should also offer to help with the dishes, but do not insist if the host refuses.

When you are dining at a restaurant or a bar, you should wait to be seated by the staff, unless it is a casual or self-service place. You should also wait for everyone to receive their food before you start eating, and eat with a knife and fork, unless you are eating finger food or a typical dish, such as gallo pinto (rice and beans). You should keep your hands above the table, and not put your elbows on the table. You should also avoid talking with your mouth full, or making loud noises while eating.

When you are ordering your food or drink, you should use polite and respectful language, and avoid slang or jokes that may offend or embarrass others. You should also use the phrase "por favor, regálame ..." (please, give me the gift of ...), which shows excellent manners and gratitude. For example: "Por favor, regálame un café" (Please, give me the gift of a coffee). You should also be careful with the hot sauce, or "salsa picante", as it may be spicier than you expect. You should also be aware that the sour cream, or "natilla", is thinner and less flavorful than you may be used to.

When you are paying the bill, you should know that most restaurants and bars include a 10% service charge and a 13% sales tax in the bill. You can leave an additional tip of 5-10% if you are happy with the service, or none if you are not. You can tip in colones or dollars, but preferably in cash. You should also know that it is customary for the person who invited the guests to pay the bill, unless otherwise agreed. You should also avoid splitting the bill, as it may be considered rude or cheap.

When you are saying goodbye, you should thank the host or the staff for their service and attention, and wish them a good day or night. You can also use the phrase "pura vida" (pure life), which is a typical Costa Rican expression that can mean anything positive. For example: "Gracias, pura vida" (Thanks, pure life).

## *Dress Code and Fashion*

Costa Rica has a relaxed and casual dress code, but also a sense of style and elegance. Costa Ricans, or Ticos, like to dress in good and clean clothing, always appropriate for the occasion and the weather. Whether you are visiting the city, the beach, or the mountains, you will find a variety of clothing options that suit your needs and preferences. Below are some of the tips and information that you should know about dress code and fashion in Costa Rica:

**For the city**: If you are visiting the capital city of San José, or other urban areas, you will find that most people dress in jeans, t-shirts, and sneakers, or other comfortable and casual outfits. However, you may also see some people wearing more formal or trendy clothing, especially for business, nightlife, or special events. You should also dress appropriately for the religious or official settings, such as churches, museums, or government offices, and avoid revealing or sloppy clothing. You should also bring a light jacket or sweater, as the temperatures can be cooler and wetter in the city.

**For the beach**: If you are visiting the coastal areas, such as Guanacaste, Puntarenas, or Limón, you will find that most people dress in shorts, tank tops, and sandals, or other light and breezy outfits. You can also wear your swimsuit, sunglasses, and hat, but make sure to cover up when you are not on the beach, as some places may not allow bare skin or wet clothing. You should also bring sun protection, such as sunscreen, lip balm, and aloe vera, as the sun can be very strong and hot on the beach.

**For the mountains**: If you are visiting the mountainous areas, such as Monteverde, Arenal, or Poás, you will find that most people dress in long pants, shirts, and closed-toe shoes, or other warm and sturdy outfits. You should also bring a rain jacket, a fleece, and a hat, as the temperatures can be colder and rainier in the mountains. You should also bring insect repellent, a flashlight, and a water bottle, as you may encounter bugs, darkness, and dehydration in the mountains.

Costa Rica is a country that has a diverse and vibrant fashion scene, influenced by its indigenous, European, African, and Asian heritage. You can find a variety of clothing styles, colors, and patterns, that reflect the culture and the nature of the country. You can also find some traditional and regional costumes, that are worn during festivals and celebrations, such as Semana Santa, Fiesta de la Virgen de los Ángeles, or Limon Carnaval. These costumes usually consist of colorful skirts, blouses, hats, and accessories, that feature the country's wildlife and folklore.

## *Festivals and Celebrations*

Below are some of the most popular and colorful festivals and celebrations that you can enjoy in this amazing country:

**Fiestas Palmares**: This is one of the largest and most anticipated festivals in Costa Rica, held every January in the town of Palmares, in the province of Alajuela. The festival features a variety of activities, such as horse parades, carnivals, concerts, bullfights, and fireworks. The festival attracts thousands of locals and tourists, who come to enjoy the festive atmosphere and the lively entertainment.

**Fiesta de la Virgen del Mar**: This is a religious and maritime festival, held every July in the port town of Puntarenas, in the province of Puntarenas. The festival honors the patron saint of sailors and fishermen, the

Virgin of the Sea, with a boat parade, a mass, and a fair. The festival also celebrates the culture and cuisine of the Pacific coast, with music, dance, and seafood.

**Fiesta de los Diablitos**: This is a cultural and ancestral festival, held every December and January in the indigenous territories of Boruca and Rey Curré, in the province of Puntarenas. The festival reenacts the historical resistance of the native people against the Spanish colonizers, with a symbolic battle between the diablitos (little devils) and the toro (bull). The festival also showcases the art and craftsmanship of the indigenous communities, with masks, costumes, and sculptures.

**Limon Carnaval**: This is a Caribbean-style carnival, held every October in the city of Limon, in the province of Limon. The carnival celebrates the Afro-Caribbean culture and heritage of the region, with parades, costumes, music, and dancing. The carnival also features a beauty pageant, a food festival, and a concert.

**Festival Internacional de las Artes**: This is an international festival of arts, held every March or April in the capital city of San José, in the province of San José. The festival showcases the artistic and creative talent of Costa Rica and other countries, with performances, exhibitions, and workshops. The festival covers a wide range of disciplines, such as theater, dance, music, cinema, literature, and visual arts.

These are just some of the many festivals and celebrations that you can find in Costa Rica, each with its own charm and flavor. By attending these events, you will be able to experience the pura vida (pure life) of Costa Rica, and learn more about its people and culture.

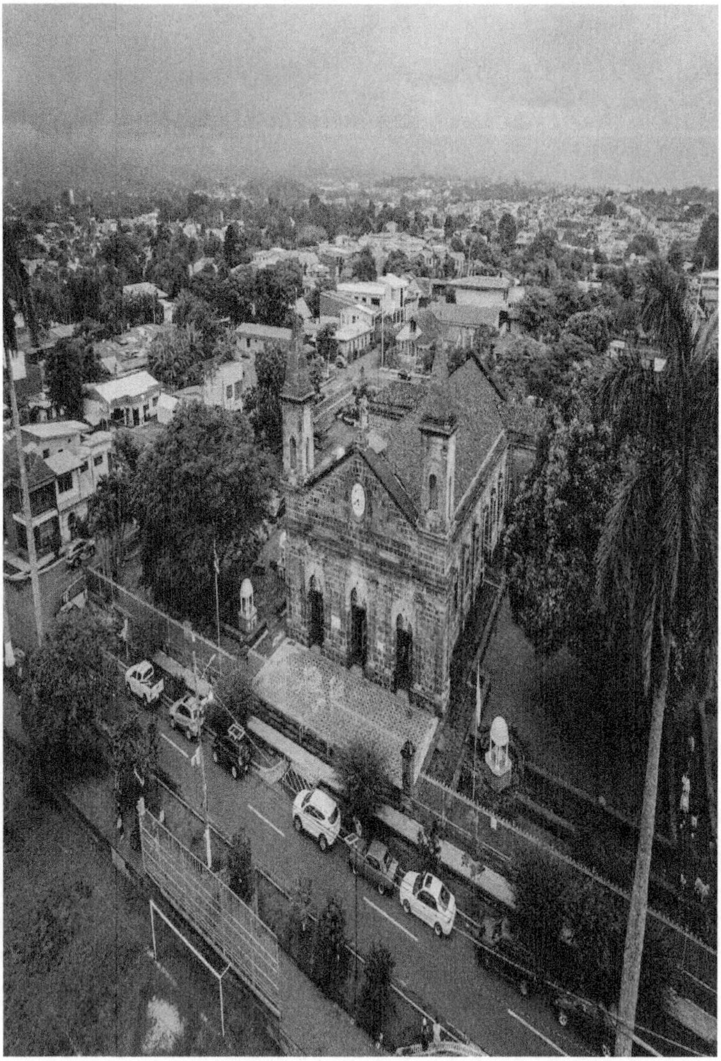

# Chapter 4 • Exploring Costa Rica's Neighbourhoods

## *The Central Valley*

The Central Valley is the heart and soul of Costa Rica, where you can experience the rich culture, history, and nature of this diverse and beautiful country. Whether you are looking for urban attractions, rural charm, or volcanic wonders, the Central Valley has something for everyone. Below are some of the highlights of this region that you should not miss on your trip to Costa Rica.

**San José:** The capital city of Costa Rica is a vibrant and cosmopolitan hub, where you can find some of the best museums, restaurants, nightlife, and shopping in the country. You can visit the National Theatre, a stunning neoclassical building that hosts cultural events and performances, or explore the Gold Museum, the Jade Museum, the National Museum, and the Children's Museum, where you can learn about the history, art, and culture of Costa Rica. San José is also a great base to explore the surrounding areas, as it has easy access to public transportation and tours.

**Poás Volcano National Park**: One of the most visited national parks in Costa Rica, Poás Volcano offers an impressive view of its active crater, which is one of the largest in the world. You can also hike to the Botos Lagoon, a beautiful turquoise lake that fills an extinct crater, or enjoy the cloud forest and the wildlife that inhabit the park. Poás Volcano is only an hour away from San José, making it a perfect day trip destination.

**Turrialba**: If you are looking for adventure and nature, Turrialba is the place for you. This town is famous for its whitewater rafting, kayaking, and mountain biking opportunities, as well as its coffee and cheese production. You can also visit the Turrialba Volcano, which is currently active and offers a spectacular sight of ash and steam, or the Guayabo National Monument, which is the largest and most important archaeological site in Costa Rica, dating back to pre-Columbian times.

**Orosi Valley**: One of the most scenic and peaceful valleys in Costa Rica, Orosi Valley is a paradise for nature lovers and history buffs. You can admire the lush green hills, the coffee plantations, the waterfalls, and the hot springs that dot the valley, or visit the Orosi Church, the oldest colonial church in Costa Rica that is still in use. You can also explore the Tapantí National Park, which protects a large area of rainforest and wildlife, or the Lankester Botanical Garden, which showcases a variety of orchids and other tropical plants.

**Valle de los Santos (Valley of the Saints):** Another picturesque valley in the Central Valley, Valle de los Santos is known for its high-quality coffee and its charming towns. You can visit Santa María de Dota, San Marcos de Tarrazú, and San Pablo de León Cortés, where you can taste some of the best coffee in the world, learn about the coffee production process, and interact with the friendly locals. You can also enjoy the stunning views of the mountains, the rivers, and the forests that surround the valley.

## *The Central Pacific Coast*

The Central Pacific Coast is a region of Costa Rica that offers a variety of attractions and activities for travelers of all tastes and preferences. Whether you are looking for sun, surf, wildlife, or culture, you will find it here. Below are some of the main features of this region that you should know before you plan your trip.

The Central Pacific Coast is located between the capital city of San José and the southern Pacific Coast. It is easily accessible by car, bus, or plane, and has a range of accommodation options, from luxury resorts to budget hostels.

The Central Pacific Coast is home to some of the most popular and beautiful beaches in Costa Rica, such as Jacó, Hermosa, Esterillos, Manuel Antonio, and Uvita. You can enjoy swimming, surfing, kayaking, snorkeling, fishing, or just relaxing on the sand. Some of the beaches are also part of national parks or marine reserves, where you can observe and protect the diverse marine life, such as whales, dolphins, turtles, and coral reefs.

The Central Pacific Coast is also rich in natural and cultural heritage, as it has several national parks, wildlife refuges, archaeological sites, and historical monuments. You can visit the Poás Volcano National Park, where you can see one of the largest active craters in the world, or the Carara National Park, where you can spot scarlet macaws, crocodiles, and other wildlife. You can also explore the Guayabo National Monument, which is the largest and most important pre-Columbian site in Costa Rica, or the Orosi Church, which is the oldest colonial church in the country.

The Central Pacific Coast is not only a place to enjoy nature, but also a place to experience the culture and lifestyle of Costa Rica. You can visit the towns and villages along the coast, where you can taste the local cuisine, coffee, and cheese, as well as interact with the friendly and hospitable people. You can also enjoy the nightlife, shopping, and entertainment options in places like San José, Jacó, and Manuel Antonio, where you can find bars, clubs, restaurants, and casinos.

## *The Guanacaste Province*

The Guanacaste Province is a region of Costa Rica that offers a unique combination of natural beauty, cultural heritage, and adventure. It is the second largest province in the country, with an area of 10,140.71 km$^2$, and the most sparsely populated. It is located in the northwestern part of the country, along the coast of the Pacific Ocean, and bordered by Nicaragua to the north, Alajuela Province to the east, and Puntarenas Province to the southeast. The province is named after the guanacaste tree, which is the national tree of Costa Rica.

The Guanacaste Province is known for its cattle ranches and spectacular beaches, as well as its volcanoes, wildlife, and archaeological sites. It is the driest region of Costa Rica, with a tropical dry forest climate that varies from hot and humid to cool and rainy depending on the elevation and season. The province has a rich and diverse culture, influenced by the indigenous Chorotega, the Spanish colonizers, the African slaves, and the Nicaraguan immigrants. The province celebrates its annexation to Costa Rica from Nicaragua on July 25th, 1824, with a holiday called Guanacaste Day.

Some of the main attractions and activities that you can enjoy in the Guanacaste Province are:

**Liberia**: The capital and largest city of the province, Liberia is a charming and historic town that serves as a gateway to the rest of the region. You can visit the colonial buildings, the museums, the churches, and the markets, or enjoy the nightlife, the restaurants, and the shopping. Liberia also has an international airport that connects the province with the rest of the country and the world.

**Beaches**: The province has some of the most popular and beautiful beaches in Costa Rica, such as Jacó, Hermosa, Esterillos, Manuel Antonio, and Uvita. You can enjoy swimming, surfing, kayaking, snorkeling, fishing, or just relaxing on the sand. Some of the beaches are also part of national parks or marine reserves, where you can observe and protect the diverse marine life, such as whales, dolphins, turtles, and coral reefs.

**Volcanoes**: The province is bounded on the east by a group of green-swathed volcanoes forming the Cordillera de Guanacaste and the Cordillera de Tilarán. You can visit the Poás Volcano National Park, where you can see one of the largest active craters in the world, or the Rincón de la Vieja National Park, where you can hike to the waterfalls, the hot springs, the mud pots, and the fumaroles. You can also explore the Miravalles Volcano, the Tenorio Volcano, and the Orosi Volcano, which offer stunning views and diverse ecosystems.

**Wildlife**: The province is home to a variety of wildlife, both on land and in the water. You can visit the Carara National Park, where you can spot scarlet macaws, crocodiles, and other animals, or the Palo Verde National Park, where you can see hundreds of bird species, monkeys, deer, and more. You can also visit the Ostional Wildlife Refuge, where you can witness the mass nesting of olive ridley sea turtles, or the Las Baulas National Marine Park, where you can see the endangered leatherback sea turtles.

**Culture**: The province has a rich and diverse culture, influenced by the indigenous Chorotega, the Spanish colonizers, the African slaves, and the Nicaraguan immigrants. You can visit the Guayabo National

Monument, which is the largest and most important pre-Columbian site in Costa Rica, dating back to 1000 BC, or the Orosi Church, which is the oldest colonial church in the country, built in 1743. You can also enjoy the music, the dance, the food, and the crafts of the province, such as the marimba, the folkloric ballet, the tortillas, and the pottery.

## *The Nicoya Peninsula*

The Nicoya Peninsula is a region of Costa Rica that offers a unique combination of natural beauty, cultural heritage, and adventure. It is the second largest peninsula in the country, with an area of 10,140.71 km², and the most sparsely populated. It is located in the northwestern part of the country, along the coast of the Pacific Ocean, and bordered by Nicaragua to the north, Alajuela Province to the east, and Puntarenas Province to the southeast. The peninsula is named after the guanacaste tree, which is the national tree of Costa Rica.

The Nicoya Peninsula is known for its cattle ranches and spectacular beaches, as well as its volcanoes, wildlife, and archaeological sites. It is the driest region of Costa Rica, with a tropical dry forest climate that varies from hot and humid to cool and rainy depending on the elevation and season. The peninsula has a rich and diverse culture, influenced by the indigenous Chorotega, the Spanish colonizers, the African slaves, and the Nicaraguan immigrants. The peninsula celebrates its annexation to Costa Rica from Nicaragua on July 25th, 1824, with a holiday called Guanacaste Day.

Some of the main attractions and activities that you can enjoy in the Nicoya Peninsula are:

**Beaches**: The province has some of the most popular and beautiful beaches in Costa Rica, such as Santa Teresa, Malpais, Montezuma, Samara, and Nosara. You can enjoy swimming, surfing, kayaking, snorkeling, fishing, or just relaxing on the sand. Some of the beaches are also part of national parks or marine reserves, where you can observe and protect the diverse marine life, such as whales, dolphins, turtles, and coral reefs. The best beaches on the Nicoya Peninsula are lauded for their seclusion and laid-back ambiance. Some of the region's beaches have been discovered by surfers who are opening up hidden sections of gorgeous shoreline.

**Volcanoes**: The province is bounded on the east by a group of green-swathed volcanoes forming the Cordillera de Guanacaste and the Cordillera de Tilarán. You can visit the Poás Volcano National Park, where you can see one of the largest active craters in the world, or the Rincón de la Vieja National Park, where you can hike to the waterfalls, the hot springs, the mud pots, and the fumaroles. You can also explore the Miravalles Volcano, the Tenorio Volcano, and the Orosi Volcano, which offer stunning views and diverse ecosystems.

**Wildlife**: The province is home to a variety of wildlife, both on land and in the water. You can visit the Carara National Park, where you can spot scarlet macaws, crocodiles, and other animals, or the Palo Verde National Park, where you can see hundreds of bird species, monkeys, deer, and more. You can also visit the Ostional Wildlife Refuge, where you can witness the mass nesting of olive ridley sea turtles, or the Las Baulas National Marine Park, where you can see the endangered leatherback sea turtles.

**Culture**: The province has a rich and diverse culture, influenced by the indigenous Chorotega, the Spanish colonizers, the African slaves, and the Nicaraguan immigrants. You can visit the Guayabo National Monument, which is the largest and most important pre-Columbian site in Costa Rica, dating back to 1000 BC, or the Orosi Church, which is the oldest colonial church in the country, built in 1743. You can also enjoy the music, the dance, the food, and the crafts of the province, such as the marimba, the folkloric ballet, the tortillas, and the pottery.

## *The Northern Plains*

The Northern Plains is a region of Costa Rica that offers a variety of attractions and activities for travelers who love nature, adventure, and culture. It is located in the north-central part of the country, between the Cordillera de Guanacaste and the Cordillera de Tilarán, and bordered by Nicaragua to the north and the Central Pacific Coast to the west. The region is characterized by its wet and evergreen forests, its fertile plains, its lakes, lagoons, volcanoes, rivers, and waterfalls, and its rich biodiversity and heritage. Below are some of the highlights of this region that you should not miss on your trip to Costa Rica.

**Arenal Volcano National Park and La Fortuna:** The Arenal Volcano is one of the most active and impressive volcanoes in the world, with constant eruptions of lava and ash that create a spectacular sight. The volcano is surrounded by lush vegetation that hosts a variety of wildlife, such as monkeys, toucans, sloths, and coatis. The park also offers hiking trails, waterfalls, hot springs, and scenic views. La Fortuna is the nearest town to the volcano, and a popular tourist destination with many hotels, restaurants, shops, and services. La Fortuna is also a great base to explore the surrounding areas, such as the Chato Hill, the Fortuna Waterfall, the Maleku Indigenous Reserve, and the Arenal Lake.

**Celeste River and Tenorio Volcano National Park**: The Celeste River is one of the natural wonders of Costa Rica, with a unique turquoise color that results from the chemical reaction of two rivers with different mineral content from the slopes of the Tenorio Volcano. The river is located within the Tenorio Volcano National Park, which protects a large area of rainforest and wildlife, as well as the Tenorio Volcano, which has four craters and a cloud forest. The park offers a trail of 7 kilometers that follows the river and showcases its main attractions, such as the Teñideros, where the river changes color, the Celeste Waterfall, the hot springs, the mud pots, and the fumaroles.

**Sarapiquí**: Sarapiquí is a canton and a river in the Northern Plains, known for its rich biodiversity and its scientific research. The region is home to several protected areas, such as the Braulio Carrillo National Park, the La Selva Biological Station, the Tirimbina

Rainforest Center, and the Sarapiquí Conservation Learning Center, where you can learn about the flora and fauna of the area, as well as the conservation efforts and the community projects. Sarapiquí is also a paradise for adventure lovers, as you can enjoy activities such as rafting, kayaking, zip-lining, horseback riding, and birdwatching.

**Caño Negro Wildlife Refuge and Río Frío:** The Caño Negro Wildlife Refuge is one of the most important wetlands in Costa Rica, and a Ramsar site of international importance. The refuge protects a variety of habitats, such as marshes, lagoons, rivers, and forests, and hosts a large number of species, such as crocodiles, turtles, caimans, monkeys, sloths, bats, and fish. The refuge is especially famous for its birdlife, with more than 350 species, including migratory and endangered ones, such as the jabiru, the roseate spoonbill, the wood stork, and the great green macaw. The Río Frío is the main river that flows through the refuge, and the best way to explore it is by boat tours that depart from the town of Los Chiles.

**Guayabo National Monument:** The Guayabo National Monument is the largest and most important archaeological site in Costa Rica, dating back to 1000

BC. The site covers an area of 218 hectares, and contains the remains of a pre-Columbian city that was inhabited by up to 10,000 people. The site features stone structures, such as roads, bridges, aqueducts, tombs, petroglyphs, and mounds, that demonstrate the advanced engineering and artistic skills of the ancient inhabitants. The site also preserves a secondary forest that attracts many birds and animals. The site is located near the town of Turrialba, and can be visited by guided tours.

## *The Southern Pacific Zone*

The Southern Pacific Zone is a region of Costa Rica that offers a unique combination of natural beauty, cultural heritage, and adventure. It is located in the south-western part of the country, along the coast of the Pacific Ocean, and bordered by the Central Pacific Coast to the north and Panama to the south. The region is characterized by its lush rainforest, spectacular biodiversity, and generally little development, making it feel like a wild jungle. Below are some of the main features of this region that you should know before you plan your trip.

**Beaches**: The region has some of the most secluded

and beautiful beaches in Costa Rica, such as Dominical, Uvita, Ojochal, Drake Bay, and Corcovado. You can enjoy swimming, surfing, kayaking, snorkeling, fishing, or just relaxing on the sand. Some of the beaches are also part of national parks or marine reserves, where you can observe and protect the diverse marine life, such as whales, dolphins, turtles, and coral reefs. The best beaches on the Southern Pacific Zone are lauded for their seclusion and laid-back ambiance. Some of the region's beaches have been discovered by surfers who are opening up hidden sections of gorgeous shoreline.

**National Parks**: The region is home to some of the most impressive and diverse national parks in Costa Rica, such as the Manuel Antonio National Park, the Marino Ballena National Park, the Corcovado National Park, and the Piedras Blancas National Park. These parks protect a variety of habitats, such as mangroves, beaches, islands, rainforest, and mountains, and host a large number of species, such as monkeys, sloths, tapirs, jaguars, macaws, and hummingbirds. The parks offer hiking trails, camping sites, ranger stations, and guided tours.

**Culture**: The region has a rich and diverse culture, influenced by the indigenous Boruca, the Spanish colonizers, the African slaves, and the Panamanian immigrants. You can visit the Boruca Indigenous Reserve, where you can learn about the history, art, and traditions of the Boruca people, who are famous for their colorful masks and textiles. You can also enjoy the music, the dance, the food, and the crafts of the region, such as the cimarrona, the bomba, the patacón, and the chicha.

## *The Caribbean Coast*

The Caribbean Coast is a region of Costa Rica that offers a unique combination of natural beauty, cultural heritage, and adventure. It is located in the eastern part of the country, along the coast of the Caribbean Sea, and bordered by Nicaragua to the north and Panama to the south. The region is characterized by its tropical rainforest, spectacular biodiversity, and generally little development, making it feel like a wild jungle. Below are some of the main features of this region that you should know before you plan your trip.

**Tortuguero**: Tortuguero, the Costa Rican version of the Amazon rainforest, dominates the northern coast of the region. This massive area is a series of rivers and canals that crisscross the jungle. Not surprisingly, it rains here often. Although the beaches are beautiful, a full day of sunny beach weather is rare. To top it off, the currents are strong and toothy barracudas and sharks roam the waters so you won't do much swimming anyways. The biggest draw here is the large numbers of turtles (hence "Tortuguero," which means "region of turtles" in Spanish) that come to nest along the shoreline. The best time to see them nesting is in April and May. But, even during the off-season, Tortuguero offers a few places to go hiking, lots of canal cruises, and an abundance of wildlife (this area is known for its birds). Tortuguero is not easy to get to nor is it cheap. It takes five hours to get there from San José and supplies are brought in by boat. Hence, it's not a budget destination. But, if it's something remote you're looking for in Central America, Tortuguero's the place to go! You can visit the Tortuguero National Park, where you can see the turtles and other animals, or take a boat tour to explore the canals and the jungle.

**Cahuita**: Cahuita is a small town on the southern coast of the region, known for its laid-back vibe and its Afro-Caribbean culture. The town has a few restaurants, bars, shops, and hotels, but the main attraction is the Cahuita National Park, which protects a coral reef, a beach, and a rainforest. The park is free to enter, and you can snorkel, swim, hike, or relax on the sand. The park is also home to many animals, such as monkeys, sloths, raccoons, and coatis. Cahuita is a great place to experience the Caribbean culture of Costa Rica, with its music, food, and language. You can also visit the nearby Aviarios del Caribe Sloth Sanctuary, where you can see and learn about these adorable creatures.

**Puerto Viejo**: Puerto Viejo is the most popular and lively town on the Caribbean coast, with a mix of locals, expats, and tourists. The town has a lot of options for accommodation, dining, nightlife, and shopping, as well as a vibrant and colorful atmosphere. Puerto Viejo is also a paradise for surfers, as it has some of the best waves in the country, especially at Salsa Brava, a reef break that attracts experienced surfers. Puerto Viejo is also a good base to explore the nearby beaches, such as Cocles, Punta Uva, and Manzanillo, which are quieter and more scenic. You can also visit the Gandoca-Manzanillo Wildlife Refuge, which protects a wetland, a mangrove, and a rainforest, and hosts a variety of wildlife, such as dolphins, manatees, turtles, and birds .

## *The Isla del Coco*

The Isla del Coco, or Cocos Island, is a remote and stunning island in the Pacific Ocean, administered by Costa Rica. It is a UNESCO World Heritage Site and a Ramsar Wetland of International Importance, as well as a national park and a district of Puntarenas Province. The island is about 550 km (342 mi) southwest of the Costa Rican mainland, and has an area of about 24 km² (9.3 sq mi). It is the only landmass above water on the Cocos tectonic plate, and the southernmost point of geopolitical North America if non-continental islands are included.

The island is famous for its natural beauty and rich biodiversity, especially its marine life. It is surrounded by deep waters with counter-currents, which create ideal conditions for an abundance of large marine species, such as hammerhead sharks, rays, dolphins, whales, turtles, and coral reefs. The island is also home to many endemic and endangered species, such as the Cocos cuckoo, the Cocos finch, the Cocos flycatcher, and the Cocos gecko. The island has a wet and evergreen climate, with a tropical rainforest that covers most of the terrain. The island also has many waterfalls, streams, and caves that add to its scenic appeal.

The island is not open to the public, and has no permanent inhabitants other than Costa Rican park rangers. The only way to visit the island is by boat, which usually takes 36 to 48 hours from the mainland. The island can only be explored by guided tours, which are limited and regulated by the park authorities. The main activities on the island are hiking, camping, and scuba diving, which are considered some of the best in the world. The island also has an information center, a park ranger's station, trails, signage, restroom services, potable water, and several lookout points.

The island has a long and fascinating history, as it was discovered by Spanish explorers in the 16th century, and was used as a base for pirates, privateers, whalers, and treasure hunters. The island has been the subject of many legends and stories, such as the one of the Treasure of Lima, a large stash of gold and jewels that was supposedly buried on the island by a British captain in 1820. The island has also inspired many writers and filmmakers, such as Robert Louis Stevenson, who based his novel Treasure Island on the island, and Michael Crichton, who featured the island in his novel Jurassic Park.

# Chapter 5 • Top Attractions

## *Manuel Antonio National Park*

Manuel Antonio National Park is one of the most popular and beautiful national parks in Costa Rica, located on the Pacific coast, south of the city of Quepos. The park covers an area of 683 hectares of land and 55,000 hectares of marine territory, and protects a variety of habitats, such as rainforest, beaches, coral reefs, islands, and mangroves. The park is home to a rich biodiversity of flora and fauna, including many endemic and endangered species, such as the squirrel monkey, the white-faced monkey, the sloth, the coati, the toucan, the macaw, and the hummingbird. The park also offers stunning views of the ocean and the mountains, as well as many activities for visitors, such as hiking, camping, swimming, snorkeling, and scuba diving.

The park was established in 1972, after a long struggle between conservationists and developers, who wanted to exploit the area for tourism and agriculture. The park was named after Manuel Antonio, a local fisherman who helped the conservationists and donated part of his land to the park. The park is now one of the main attractions of Costa Rica, receiving more than 400,000 visitors per year. The park is open every day except on Tuesdays, from 7:00 am to 4:00 pm, and the entrance fee is $18.08 for adults and $5.65 for children. The park has an information center, a ranger station, trails, signs, restrooms, potable water, and several lookout points. The park also offers guided tours, which are recommended to learn more about the park's history, ecology, and wildlife.

The park has four main beaches, which are considered among the most beautiful in the country. They are:

**Manuel Antonio Beach:** This is the main and most popular beach in the park, located at the end of the main trail. It has white sand, clear water, and calm waves, ideal for swimming and relaxing. It also has a view of the Cathedral Point, a rocky formation that separates the beach from the Espadilla Sur Beach. The beach has some facilities, such as showers, restrooms, and picnic tables, but no food or drinks are allowed. The beach is also frequented by monkeys and raccoons, who may try to steal your belongings, so be careful and do not feed them.

**Espadilla Sur Beach:** This is the second largest and

most visited beach in the park, located next to the Manuel Antonio Beach. It has golden sand, turquoise water, and moderate waves, suitable for swimming and surfing. It also has a view of the Cathedral Point and the islands of the park. The beach has some facilities, such as showers, restrooms, and picnic tables, but no food or drinks are allowed. The beach is also home to many animals, such as monkeys, sloths, iguanas, and crabs.

**Playita Beach**: This is a small and secluded beach in the park, located behind Cathedral Point. It has dark sand, clear water, and strong waves, ideal for surfing and snorkelling. It also has a view of the islands of the park and the Manuel Antonio Beach. The beach has no facilities, and no food or drinks are allowed. The beach is also a popular spot for nudists, although nudity is not officially permitted in the park.

**Playa Gemelas**: This is a small and quiet beach in the park, located at the end of a secondary trail. It has white sand, green water, and gentle waves, perfect for swimming and sunbathing. It also has a view of the islands of the park and the Playita Beach. The beach has no facilities, and no food or drinks are allowed. The beach is also a good place to see birds, such as pelicans, herons, and egrets.

## *Arenal Volcano*

Arenal Volcano is one of the most amazing and exciting destinations in Costa Rica, where you can experience the beauty and power of nature. Arenal Volcano is a cone-shaped active volcano that rises 1,670 meters (5,480 feet) above sea level, and is located in the northwestern part of the country, about 90 kilometers (56 miles) from the capital city of San José. Arenal Volcano is surrounded by the Arenal Volcano National Park, which covers an area of 29,692 hectares (73,352 acres) of rainforest, lakes, rivers, and waterfalls. Arenal Volcano is also the centerpiece of a region that offers a variety of attractions and activities for all kinds of travelers, from adventure seekers to nature lovers.

Some of the best things to do at Arenal Volcano are:

**Hiking**: You can explore the trails of the Arenal Volcano National Park, which offer different levels of difficulty and length, and allow you to see the volcano from different angles, as well as the flora and fauna of the area. You can also hike to the base of the volcano, where you can see the solidified lava flows and the craters from previous eruptions. You can hike on your own or with a guide, who can explain the history and ecology of the volcano and the park.

**Hot Springs**: You can relax and enjoy the natural hot springs that are heated by the geothermal activity of the volcano. There are several hot springs resorts in the area, such as Tabacon, Baldi, and The Springs, which offer pools of different temperatures, sizes, and shapes, as well as amenities such as spas, restaurants, and bars. The hot springs are a perfect way to soothe your muscles and mind after a day of adventure.

**Zip-lining:** You can experience the thrill of flying over the rainforest canopy on a zip-line tour, which is one of the most popular activities in the area. You can choose from different zip-line operators, such as Sky Adventures, Arenal Mundo Aventura, and Ecoglide, which offer different lengths, heights, and speeds of zip-lines, as well as other features such as hanging bridges, rappelling, and tarzan swings. Zip-lining is a fun and safe way to enjoy the views of the volcano and the forest, and to spot some wildlife along the way.

**Wildlife Tours**: You can discover the amazing biodiversity of the region on a wildlife tour, which can be done by boat, kayak, horseback, or on foot. You can visit places such as the Caño Negro Wildlife Refuge, the Palo Verde National Park, the La Fortuna Waterfall, and the

Arenal Lake, where you can see a variety of animals, such as monkeys, sloths, crocodiles, turtles, birds, and fish. You can also visit the Arenal Natura Ecological Park, where you can see reptiles, amphibians, insects, and butterflies in their natural habitats.

**Cultural Tours**: You can learn about the culture and history of the region on a cultural tour, which can include visits to local towns, farms, markets, and museums. You can also experience the cuisine, music, and art of the region, such as the tortillas, the coffee, the cacao, the marimba, and the pottery. You can also visit the Maleku Indigenous Reserve, where you can meet the indigenous people who live in the area and learn about their traditions and customs.

## *Monteverde Cloud Forest Biological Reserve*

Monteverde Cloud Forest Biological Reserve is one of the most amazing and beautiful places to visit in Costa Rica, where you can experience the wonders of nature and the diversity of life. Monteverde Cloud Forest Biological Reserve is a private reserve that covers an area of 10,500 hectares (25,950 acres) of cloud forest, a rare and fragile ecosystem that only covers 1% of the world's forests. The reserve is located in the Cordillera de Tilarán, between the provinces of Puntarenas and Alajuela, and is part of the larger Monteverde Conservation Area, which includes other reserves and biological corridors.

The reserve was founded in 1972 by a group of scientists from the Tropical Science Center and a community of Quakers who settled in the area in the 1950s. The reserve's main goal is to protect the cloud forest and its biodiversity, as well as to promote scientific research and environmental education. The reserve is open to the public every day from 7:00 am to 4:00 pm, and the entrance fee is $25 for non-national adults, $12 for non-national children, $8 for citizen/resident adults, and $6 for citizen/resident children. The reserve has an information center, a ranger station, trails, signs, restrooms, potable water, and several lookout points. The reserve also offers guided tours, which are recommended to learn more about the park's history, ecology, and wildlife.

The reserve has a lot to offer for visitors who love nature and adventure. Some of the best things to do at Monteverde Cloud Forest Biological Reserve are:

**Hiking**: You can explore the trails of the reserve, which range from easy to difficult, and allow you to see the cloud forest from different perspectives, as well as the flora and fauna of the area. You can also hike to the Continental Divide, where you can see both the Pacific and the Caribbean coasts on a clear day. You can hike on your own or with a guide, who can explain the history and ecology of the cloud forest and the reserve.

**Birdwatching**: You can enjoy the incredible diversity of birds that inhabit the cloud forest, which include more than 400 species, such as the resplendent quetzal, the three-wattled bellbird, the hummingbird, and the toucan. You can also see other animals, such as monkeys, sloths, coatis, and agoutis. The best time to see the birds is early in the morning or late in the afternoon, when they are more active. You can use binoculars, cameras, or telescopes to get a better view of the birds, and you can also listen to their songs and calls.

**Zip-lining**: You can experience the thrill of flying over the cloud forest canopy on a zip-line tour, which is one of the most popular activities in the area. You can choose from different zip-line operators, such as Sky Trek, Selvatura, and 100% Aventura, which offer different lengths, heights, and speeds of zip-lines, as well as other features such as hanging bridges, tarzan swings, and bungee jumping. Zip-lining is a fun and safe way to enjoy the views of the cloud forest and the mountains, and to spot some wildlife along the way.

**Coffee and Chocolate Tours**: You can learn about the culture and history of coffee and chocolate in Monteverde, and taste some of the best and freshest products in the world. You can visit local farms, cooperatives, and factories, where you can see the process of growing, harvesting, roasting, and making coffee and chocolate. You can also participate in the process by picking, peeling, and grinding the beans, and making your own cup of coffee or bar of chocolate. You can also learn about the social and environmental impact of coffee and chocolate production in the area.

## *Tamarindo*

Tamarindo is a district and a town in the Guanacaste province of Costa Rica, located on the Pacific coast. It is one of the most popular and developed beach destinations in the country, offering a variety of attractions and activities for all kinds of travelers. Whether you are looking for surfing, sportfishing, diving, wildlife, culture, or nightlife, Tamarindo has something for you. Below are some of the main features of this region that you should know before you plan your trip.

**Surfing**: Tamarindo is a paradise for surfers, as it has some of the best waves and beaches in Costa Rica. You can find waves for all levels of experience, from beginners to experts, and enjoy the warm and clear water. Some of the most famous surf spots are Playa Tamarindo, Playa Langosta, Playa Grande, and Playa Avellanas. You can also take surf lessons, rent surfboards, or join surf tours and camps.

**Sportfishing**: Tamarindo is also a great place for sportfishing, as it has access to the rich waters of the Pacific Ocean. You can catch a variety of fish, such as marlin, sailfish, tuna, dorado, wahoo, roosterfish, and snapper. You can also join fishing charters, which provide boats, equipment, guides, and snacks. You can choose from half-day, full-day, or multi-day trips, depending on your budget and preference.

**Diving**: Tamarindo is also a good base to explore the underwater world of the Pacific Ocean. You can dive or snorkel in the nearby Catalina Islands, which are a group of volcanic rocks that host a diverse marine life, such as sharks, rays, turtles, dolphins, and fish. You can also dive or snorkel in the Bat Islands, which are farther away but offer a more challenging and rewarding experience, as you can see bull sharks, manta rays, and whales. You can find several dive shops and operators in Tamarindo, which offer courses, equipment, and tours.

**Wildlife**: Tamarindo is also a place where you can see and interact with the amazing wildlife of Costa Rica. You can visit the Monkey Park, which is a wildlife rescue center that rehabilitates and releases animals, such as monkeys, sloths, raccoons, and birds. You can also visit the Tamarindo Wildlife Refuge, which protects a mangrove forest and a wetland, and hosts animals such as crocodiles, iguanas, and birds. You can also join wildlife tours, which can take you to places such as the Palo Verde National Park, the Caño Negro Wildlife Refuge, and the Rincon de la Vieja National Park, where you can see more animals, such as monkeys, sloths, crocodiles, turtles, birds, and volcanoes.

**Culture**: Tamarindo is also a place where you can learn about the culture and history of Costa Rica. You can visit local towns, farms, markets, and museums, where you can see the lifestyle, traditions, and crafts of the people. You can also experience the cuisine, music, and art of the region, such as the tortillas, the coffee, the cacao, the marimba, and the pottery. You can also visit the Maleku

Indigenous Reserve, where you can meet the indigenous people who live in the area and learn about their customs and beliefs.

## *Tortuguero National Park*

Tortuguero National Park is a national park in the Limón Province of Costa Rica, located on the Caribbean coast. It is one of the most biodiverse and ecologically important areas in the country, as it protects a variety of habitats, such as rainforest, mangrove, wetland, beach, and ocean. The park is also famous for being the nesting site of several species of sea turtles, especially the green turtle, which is endangered. The park is accessible only by boat or plane, and offers a unique and unforgettable experience of nature and wildlife.

Some of the best things to do at Tortuguero National Park are:

**Boating**: You can explore the canals and lagoons of the park by boat, which is the main way to see the park. You can join a guided tour or rent a canoe or kayak, and enjoy the scenery and the wildlife along the way. You can see animals such as monkeys, sloths, crocodiles, iguanas, and birds, as well as plants such as orchids, bromeliads, and palms. You can also visit the small town of Tortuguero, which is the gateway to the park, and learn about the culture and history of the area.

**Turtle watching:** You can witness the amazing spectacle of sea turtles nesting and hatching on the beaches of the park, which is one of the main attractions of the park. You can see four species of sea turtles: green, leatherback, hawksbill, and loggerhead, depending on the season. The nesting season runs from March to October, with the peak from July to September. The hatching season runs from May to December, with the peak from September to November. You can join a guided tour at night, which is the only way to see the turtles, and follow the rules and regulations to avoid disturbing them.

**Hiking**: You can hike the trails of the park, which offer different levels of difficulty and length, and allow you to see the rainforest and the beach from different perspectives. You can also hike to the Cerro Tortuguero, which is the highest point of the park, and enjoy the panoramic view of the park and the ocean. You can hike on your own or with a guide, who can explain the history and ecology of the park and the forest.

**Birdwatching**: You can enjoy the incredible diversity of birds that inhabit the park, which include more than

400 species, such as the great green macaw, the toucan, the hummingbird, and the kingfisher. You can also see other animals, such as monkeys, sloths, coatis, and agoutis. The best time to see the birds is early in the morning or late in the afternoon, when they are more active. You can use binoculars, cameras, or telescopes to get a better view of the birds, and you can also listen to their songs and calls.

**Fishing**: You can enjoy the sport fishing opportunities that the park offers, as it has access to the rich waters of the Caribbean Sea. You can catch a variety of fish, such as tarpon, snook, jack, and barracuda. You can also join fishing charters, which provide boats, equipment, guides, and snacks. You can choose from half-day, full-day, or multi-day trips, depending on your budget and preference.

## *La Fortuna Waterfall*

La Fortuna Waterfall is one of the most spectacular and impressive waterfalls in Costa Rica, located near the town of La Fortuna in the Arenal Volcano National Park. The waterfall is 70 meters (230 feet) high and falls into a clear pool surrounded by lush rainforest. The waterfall is a popular attraction for visitors who want to enjoy the natural beauty, swim in the refreshing water, and support a local non-profit organization that manages the area.

Some of the best things to know before visiting La Fortuna Waterfall are:

**How to get there**: The waterfall is accessible by car, bus, taxi, or bike from the town of La Fortuna, which is about 6 kilometers (3.7 miles) away. You can also join a guided tour that includes transportation and entrance fee. The road to the waterfall is paved and well-maintained, but it can be steep and curvy in some parts. There is a parking lot at the entrance of the waterfall, where you can leave your vehicle for a small fee.

**When to go**: The waterfall is open every day from 7:00 am to 5:00 pm, and the best time to visit is early in the morning or late in the afternoon, when there are fewer crowds and better light for photography. The waterfall is also affected by the weather and the seasons, so it can be more or less powerful depending on the rainfall. The dry season runs from December to April, and the rainy season runs from May to November. The rainy season can offer more water and more greenery, but also more mosquitoes and mud.

**How much it costs**: The entrance fee to the waterfall is $18 for non-national adults, $12 for non-national children, $8 for citizen/resident adults, and $6 for citizen/resident children. The fee is used to support the Integral Development Association of La Fortuna (ADIFORT), a non-profit organization that works to improve the well-being and growth of the local community through various projects, such as road infrastructure, environment, education, sport, culture, and public safety.

**What to expect**: To reach the waterfall, you have to walk down a path of about 530 steps, which takes about 15 minutes. The path is safe and comfortable, with rest areas and water stations along the way. The path also offers views of the forest and the waterfall from different angles. Once you reach the bottom, you can admire the waterfall from a spacious and convenient viewpoint, where you can take pictures and videos. You can also swim in the pool, but be careful as the water can be cold and deep, and the rocks can be slippery. There are showers, restrooms, and changing rooms available at the bottom. To go back up, you have to climb the same steps, which can be tiring but rewarding.

**What to bring**: You should bring comfortable shoes,

water, sunscreen, insect repellent, swimsuit, towel, and a waterproof bag or case for your valuables. You should also bring cash, as there are no ATMs or credit card machines at the entrance. You should not bring food or drinks, as they are not allowed in the area. You should also not bring pets, as they are not allowed either.

## *Teatro Nacional Costa Rica*

Teatro Nacional Costa Rica is the national theatre of Costa Rica, and one of the most historic and elegant buildings in the capital city of San José. It was built in 1897 with a tax on coffee exports, and it opened with a performance of Faust by Goethe. The theatre has a neo-classical style, with statues of Calderón de la Barca and Beethoven on the front, and a mural by Villa on the inside. The theatre is a cultural and tourist attraction, as it hosts high-quality performances of theatre, opera, ballet, and music, as well as guided tours and exhibitions. The theatre is also a symbol of the country's artistic and social development, and a source of pride for the Costa Rican people.

Some of the best things to do at Teatro Nacional Costa Rica are:

**Watch a performance**: You can enjoy a variety of

shows at the theatre, from classical to contemporary, and from local to international. You can see the National Symphonic Orchestra, the National Lyric Company, the National Dance Company, and other renowned artists and groups. You can also see the theatre's own productions, such as the annual Christmas concert, the Zarzuela Festival, and the International Theatre Festival.

**Take a tour**: You can take a guided tour of the theatre, which lasts about 45 minutes and costs $10 for non-national adults and $5 for non-national children. You can see the main hall, the foyer, the auditorium, the stage, and the backstage, and learn about the history, architecture, and art of the theatre. You can also see the museum, which displays costumes, props, posters, and photographs from past shows. The tours are available every day from 9:00 am to 4:00 pm, except on Mondays and holidays.

**Visit the café**: You can relax and enjoy a coffee or a snack at the theatre's café, which is located on the ground floor. The café has a cozy and elegant atmosphere, and offers a view of the Plaza de la Cultura. You can also buy souvenirs, books, and CDs at the café's shop. The café is open every day from 9:00 am to 5:00 pm, except on Mondays and holidays.

## *Rio Celeste*

Rio Celeste is a river in the Tenorio Volcano National Park of Costa Rica, famous for its stunning turquoise color and its majestic waterfall. Rio Celeste is a natural wonder that attracts many visitors who want to enjoy the beauty and the adventure of this unique place. Below are some of the things you need to know before visiting Rio Celeste:

**How to get there**: Rio Celeste is located in the northern part of the country, about 90 kilometers (56 miles) from the capital city of San José. You can get there by car, bus, taxi, or plane. If you go by car, you need a 4x4 vehicle, as the road can be rough and muddy. You can also take a bus from San José to Guatuso, and then a taxi to the park entrance. If you prefer to fly, you can take a domestic flight from San José to La Fortuna, and then a taxi to the park entrance. You can also join a guided tour that includes transportation and entrance fee, such as this one.

**When to go**: Rio Celeste is open every day from 8:00 am to 4:00 pm, and the best time to visit is during the dry season, from December to April, when the water is more clear and blue. The rainy season, from May to

November, can make the water more cloudy and brown, due to the sediment and the runoff. However, the rainy season can also offer more greenery and wildlife, as well as fewer crowds and lower prices.

**How much it costs**: The entrance fee to the park is $12 for non-national adults and $5 for non-national children. The fee is used to support the conservation and management of the park and the river. You can pay by cash or card at the park entrance. You can also rent rubber boots for $2, as the trail can be wet and slippery.

**What to expect**: To reach the river and the waterfall, you have to hike a trail of about 7 kilometers (4.3 miles) round trip, which takes about 3 to 4 hours. The trail is moderate to difficult, with some steep and rocky sections. The trail also offers views of the forest and the river from different angles. Along the way, you can see the Teñideros, where two colorless streams mix and create the blue color of the river, due to a chemical reaction. You can also see the hot springs, where the water is heated by the volcanic activity. Once you reach the waterfall, you can admire the 30-meter (98-foot) drop of blue water into a pool below. You can also swim in the pool, but be careful as the water can be cold and deep, and the rocks can be slippery. There are showers, restrooms, and changing rooms available at the park entrance.

**What to bring**: You should bring comfortable shoes, water, sunscreen, insect repellent, swimsuit, towel, and a waterproof bag or case for your valuables. You should also bring cash, as there are no ATMs or credit card machines at the park entrance. You should not bring food or drinks, as they are not allowed in the park. You should also not bring pets, as they are not allowed either.

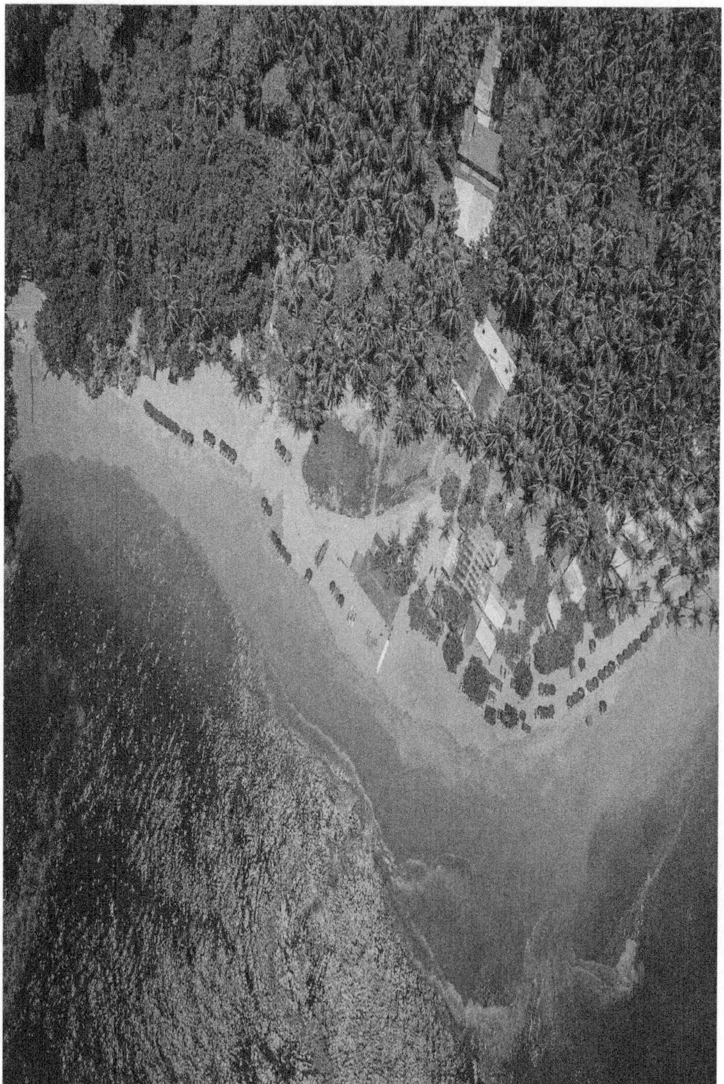

# Chapter 6 • Accommodation in Costa Rica

## *Resort Recommendations*

Below are some of the best all-inclusive resorts in Costa Rica that you can choose from:

**Four Seasons Resort Costa Rica at Peninsula Papagayo**: This is a luxury resort that offers stunning views of the Pacific Ocean and the tropical forest. You can enjoy spacious and elegant rooms, suites, or villas, some with private pools or plunge pools. The resort has four restaurants, three bars, two pools, a spa, a golf course, a fitness center, and a kids club. You can also take advantage of the many activities and excursions that the resort offers, such as canoeing, surfing, hiking, zip-lining, wildlife tours, and more.

**JW Marriott Hotel Guanacaste Resort & Spa**: This is a family-friendly resort that is located on a secluded beach in the Guanacaste province. You can choose from comfortable and stylish rooms or suites, some with ocean views or balconies. The resort has five restaurants, two bars, a pool, a spa, a fitness center, and a kids club. You can also enjoy the activities and entertainment that the resort provides, such as yoga, salsa dancing, live music, beach volleyball, horseback riding, and more.

**Planet Hollywood Costa Rica, An Autograph Collection All-Inclusive Resort**: This is a fun and trendy resort that is designed to make you feel like a star. You can stay in one of the 292 suites, some with private pools or terraces. The resort has seven restaurants, five bars, two pools, a spa, a fitness center, and a kids club. You can also experience the Hollywood memorabilia, the disco, the nightly entertainment, and the themed activities that the resort offers, such as acting, karaoke, movie nights, scavenger hunts, and more. The resort is part of the Autograph Collection, a group of unique and independent hotels that are curated by Marriott.

**Margaritaville Beach Resort Playa Flamingo:** This is a casual and laid-back resort that is inspired by the songs and lifestyle of Jimmy Buffett. You can relax in one of the cozy and colorful rooms or suites, some with ocean views or balconies. The resort has four restaurants, three bars, a pool, a spa, a fitness center, and a kids club. You can also join the fun and festive activities and events that the resort organizes, such as margarita making, trivia, bingo, karaoke, live music, and more.

## *Hotel Recommendations*

Below are some of the best hotels in Costa Rica that you can book for your trip:

**Hotel Grano de Oro**: This is a charming boutique hotel that is located in a restored Victorian mansion in the heart of San José. You can enjoy the elegant and cozy rooms, suites, or apartments, some with jacuzzi tubs or private gardens. The hotel has a restaurant, a bar, a rooftop terrace, a jacuzzi, and a spa. You can also admire the beautiful art and antiques that decorate the hotel, or visit the nearby attractions, such as the National Theater, the Jade Museum, or the Central Market.

**Nayara Gardens:** This is a luxury resort that is nestled in the Arenal Volcano National Park, surrounded by lush gardens and exotic wildlife. You can stay in one of the spacious and romantic bungalows, casitas, or villas, some with private pools or hot tubs. The resort has four restaurants, two bars, a pool, a spa, a yoga pavilion, and a fitness center. You can also enjoy the activities and tours that the resort offers, such as hiking, zip-lining, rafting, birdwatching, and more.

**Hotel Belmar:** This is a cozy and eco-friendly hotel that is located in the cloud forest of Monteverde. You can stay in one of the rustic and comfortable rooms or suites, some with balconies or terraces. The hotel has two restaurants, a bar, a pool, a spa, a yoga studio, and a juice bar. You can also appreciate the organic and sustainable practices that the hotel follows, such as using solar panels, composting, and growing their own food.

**Hotel Banana Azul**: This is a beachfront hotel that is situated in the Caribbean coast of Puerto Viejo. You can relax in one of the colorful and tropical rooms, suites, or villas, some with ocean views or hammocks. The hotel has a restaurant, a bar, a pool, a spa, a bike rental, and a tour desk. You can also explore the nearby attractions, such as the Cahuita National Park, the Jaguar Rescue Center, or the chocolate tour.

## *Villa Recommendations*

Below are some of the best villa recommendations:

**Eco-Turismo Guayacanes**: This is an eco-friendly villa that is located in Sámara, a charming beach town on the Pacific coast. You can stay in one of the four air-conditioned rooms, each with a private bathroom and a terrace. The villa has a shared kitchen, a dining area, a lounge, a garden, and a barbecue. You can also enjoy the free WiFi, the private parking, and the bicycle rental. You can explore the nearby attractions, such as the Barra Honda National Park, the Sámara Beach, or the Carrillo Beach.

**Costa Rica Villas**: This is a luxury villa that is located in Manuel Antonio, a popular tourist destination on the Pacific coast. You can choose from a variety of villas, ranging from two to eight bedrooms, some with private pools or jacuzzis. The villas have fully equipped kitchens, living rooms, dining rooms, balconies, and patios. You can also enjoy the stunning views of the ocean and the tropical forest. The villa offers a full-service package, including airport transfers, daily maid service, concierge service, and chef service. You can also take advantage of the activities and excursions that the villa offers, such as fishing, surfing, hiking, zip-lining, wildlife tours, and more.

**Villas Costa Rica**: This is a collection of villas that are located in different regions of Costa Rica, such as Guanacaste, Puntarenas, Jaco, Arenal, and Monteverde.

You can find a villa that suits your preferences, budget, and location, from beachfront villas to mountain villas. The villas have various amenities, such as pools, spas, gyms, game rooms, theaters, and event tents. The villas also offer customized packages, including personal chef services, transportation services, entertainment services, and wedding services. You can also enjoy the local attractions, such as the volcanoes, the waterfalls, the rainforests, or the beaches.

## *Hostel Recommendations*

Below are some of the best hostels in Costa Rica that you can choose from:

**Pagalù Hostel**: This is an eco-friendly hostel that is located in Puerto Viejo, a lively beach town on the Caribbean coast. You can stay in one of the four air-conditioned rooms, each with a private bathroom and a terrace. The hostel has a shared kitchen, a dining area, a lounge, a garden, and a barbecue. You can also enjoy the free WiFi, the private parking, and the bicycle rental. You can explore the nearby attractions, such as the Barra Honda National Park, the Sámara Beach, or the Carrillo Beach.

**Hostel Cattleya - Monteverde, Costa Rica**: This is

a cozy and comfortable hostel that is located in Monteverde, a cloud forest reserve that is home to many species of flora and fauna. You can stay in one of the rustic and spacious rooms, each with a seating area and a toaster. The hostel has a shared kitchen, a dining area, a lounge, a garden, and a terrace. You can also enjoy the free WiFi, the free parking, and the tour desk. You can enjoy the activities and tours that the hostel offers, such as hiking, zip-lining, birdwatching, and more.

**Pura Vibra Hostel:** This is a fun and vibrant hostel that is located in Fortuna, a town near the Arenal Volcano, one of the most active volcanoes in the world. You can stay in one of the colorful and modern rooms, some with private bathrooms and balconies. The hostel has a shared kitchen, a dining area, a lounge, a pool, and a spa. You can also enjoy the free WiFi, the free parking, and the concierge service. You can join the fun and festive activities and events that the hostel organizes, such as yoga, salsa dancing, live music, and more.

**El Clan**: This is a friendly and relaxed hostel that is located in Puerto Viejo, a lively beach town on the Caribbean coast. You can stay in one of the tropical and artistic rooms, some with private bathrooms and hammocks. The hostel has a shared kitchen, a dining area, a lounge, a pool, and a bar. You can also enjoy the free WiFi, the free parking, and the shared kitchen. You can explore the nearby attractions, such as the Cahuita National Park, the Jaguar Rescue Center, or the chocolate tour.

## Guesthouse Recommendations

Below are some of the best guesthouses in Costa Rica that you can choose from:

**Casa Garitas GuestHouse - Free SJO Airport Shuttle:** This is an eco-friendly guesthouse that is located in a quiet and beautiful neighborhood, full of lush green trees and lots of birds, yet just 5 minutes driving from the international airport and 15 minutes from downtown San José. You can enjoy spacious and elegant rooms, each with a private bathroom and a terrace. The guesthouse has a shared kitchen, a dining area, a lounge, a garden, and a barbecue. You can also enjoy the free WiFi, the private parking, and the free shuttle service to and from the airport.

**Cabañas Daneysha**: This is a charming guesthouse that is located in Tortuguero, a remote and natural paradise on the Caribbean coast, famous for its canals, wildlife, and turtle nesting. You can stay in one of the four air-conditioned rooms, each with a private bathroom and a terrace with a lake view. The guesthouse has a shared kitchen, a dining area, a lounge, a garden, and a tour desk. You can also enjoy the free WiFi, the private parking, and the bicycle rental. You can explore the nearby attractions, such as the Tortuguero National Park, the Tortuguero Village, or the Sea Turtle Conservancy.

**Casa Terraza (Casa Balbi)**: This is a cozy and comfortable guesthouse that is located in Monteverde, a cloud forest reserve that is home to many species of flora and fauna. You can stay in one of the rustic and spacious rooms, each with a seating area and a toaster. The guesthouse has a shared kitchen, a dining area, a lounge, a garden, and a terrace. You can also enjoy the free WiFi, the free parking, and the tour desk. You can enjoy the activities and tours that the guesthouse offers, such as hiking, zip-lining, birdwatching, and more.

**Casas Guaney**: This is a luxury guesthouse that is located in Manuel Antonio, a popular tourist destination on the Pacific coast, known for its beaches, wildlife, and national park. You can choose from comfortable and stylish rooms or suites, some with private bathrooms and balconies. The guesthouse has a shared kitchen, a dining area, a lounge, a pool, and a spa. You can also enjoy the stunning views of the ocean and the tropical forest. The guesthouse offers a concierge service, a car rental service, and a shuttle service. You can also take advantage of the activities and excursions that the guesthouse offers, such as fishing, surfing, hiking, zip-lining, wildlife tours, and more.

# Chapter 7 • Costa Rican Cuisine and Food Experiences

## *Introduction to Costa Rican Cuisine*

Costa Rican cuisine is a delicious and diverse blend of influences from different cultures and regions. It reflects the rich history, geography, and biodiversity of the country, as well as the creativity and hospitality of its people. In this introduction, you will learn about the origin, ingredients, and flavors of Costa Rican cuisine, and some of the most popular and traditional dishes that you can try during your visit.

Costa Rican cuisine has its roots in the indigenous cultures that inhabited the land before the Spanish colonization. Corn, beans, squash, potatoes, cassava, and fruits were the main staples of their diet, and they used various methods of cooking, such as boiling, roasting, and grinding. They also hunted and fished for meat and seafood, and gathered wild plants and herbs for seasoning.

The Spanish conquest brought new ingredients and influences to Costa Rican cuisine, such as rice, wheat, cheese, milk, meat, and spices. The Spaniards also introduced cattle, pigs, chickens, and horses, which changed the landscape and the economy of the country. The African slaves that were brought by the Spaniards also contributed to the culinary diversity of Costa Rica, especially on the Caribbean coast, where they cooked with coconut, plantains, ginger, and chili peppers.

Costa Rican cuisine also incorporates elements from other countries and regions, such as Italy, China, France, and the Middle East, as a result of immigration and globalization. However, Costa Rican cuisine still maintains its own identity and character, and it varies depending on the location and the season. For example, the cuisine of the Central Valley is influenced by the urban and cosmopolitan lifestyle of the capital, San José, while the cuisine of the Pacific coast is more seafood-based and tropical. The cuisine of the Caribbean coast is more spicy and exotic, while the cuisine of the Northern region is more influenced by the Nicaraguan culture.

Costa Rican cuisine is generally mild, fresh, and

nutritious, with a high reliance on fruits and vegetables. Rice and beans are the most common and basic ingredients, and they are often served together or separately in every meal. Costa Rican cuisine also uses a lot of herbs and spices, such as cilantro, oregano, garlic, onion, and cumin, to add flavor and aroma to the dishes. One of the most distinctive and popular condiments in Costa Rican cuisine is salsa Lizano, a brown sauce made with vegetables, vinegar, sugar, salt, and spices. It is used to season many dishes, such as gallo pinto, casado, and olla de carne.

## *Famous Costa Rican Dishes*

Some of the most famous and traditional dishes of Costa Rican cuisine are:

**Gallo pinto**: This is the national dish of Costa Rica, and it consists of rice and black or red beans, sauteed in oil with diced onions, sweet peppers, and fresh cilantro. It is usually eaten for breakfast, accompanied by eggs, cheese, tortillas, sour cream, and salsa Lizano. It can also be eaten for lunch or dinner, with meat, chicken, or fish. The name gallo pinto means "spotted rooster" in Spanish, and it refers to the speckled appearance of the rice and beans. Gallo pinto is also a symbol of the Costa

Rican culture and identity, and it is often served at special occasions and celebrations.

**Casado**: This is the most common dish for lunch and dinner in Costa Rica, and it consists of a plate with rice, beans, salad, fried plantains, and a choice of meat, chicken, fish, or cheese. The name casado means "married" in Spanish, and it refers to the combination of different ingredients that make a balanced and satisfying meal. Casado is also a reflection of the Costa Rican family values and traditions, as it is often prepared and shared by the wives and mothers of the households.

**Ceviche**: This is a popular appetizer or snack in Costa Rica, and it consists of fresh raw fish marinated in citrus juices, such as lime or lemon, with finely diced herbs and vegetables, such as cilantro, onion, sweet pepper, and chili pepper. The acid from the citrus juices "cooks" the fish, making it tender and flavorful. Ceviche is usually served cold, with crackers, tortilla chips, or patacones (fried green plantains). Ceviche is also a refreshing and healthy dish, as it is rich in protein, vitamins, and minerals.

**Olla de carne**: This is a traditional soup or stew in Costa Rica, and it consists of beef and various vegetables, such as potatoes, cassava, carrots, corn, chayote, and plantains, cooked in a broth with spices, such as bay leaves, oregano, and salt. Olla de carne is usually eaten for lunch or dinner, with rice and tortillas. Olla de carne is also a hearty and comforting dish, especially during the rainy season or the cold months.

**Sopa negra:** This is a typical soup in Costa Rica, and it consists of black beans, hard-boiled eggs, onion, garlic, cilantro, and spices, such as cumin, oregano, and salt. Sopa negra is usually eaten for lunch or dinner, with rice and tortillas. Sopa negra is also a nutritious and delicious dish, as it is high in protein, fiber, and iron.

These are just some of the amazing dishes that you can find in Costa Rican cuisine. There are many more to discover and enjoy, such as arroz con pollo, chifrijo, tamales, picadillo, and empanadas. Costa Rican cuisine is a feast for the senses, and a great way to experience the culture and the people of this wonderful country.

## *Famous Costa Rican Drinks*

Below are some of the most famous Costa Rican drinks that you should try while traveling in this beautiful country:

**Guaro**: This is the national drink of Costa Rica, and it is a clear liquor made from sugar cane. It has a mild and smooth taste, similar to vodka, and it is usually mixed with fruit juices, soda, or water to make different cocktails. Some of the most popular guaro cocktails are guaro sour, which is made with lemon juice and sugar; chiliguaro, which is made with tomato juice, lime juice, and hot sauce; and guaro con fresco, which is made with any kind of fruit juice. Guaro is also consumed as a shot, sometimes with a slice of lime or a pinch of salt. Guaro is a cheap and widely available drink in Costa Rica, and it is often served at parties and celebrations.

**Coffee**: Coffee is one of the most important and popular drinks in Costa Rica, as the country produces some of the best coffee beans in the world. Costa Rican coffee is known for its high quality, rich flavor, and aromatic scent, and it is usually brewed in a traditional way using a chorreador, which is a wooden stand with a cloth filter. Coffee is usually enjoyed in the morning with breakfast and in the afternoon with a snack, either black or with milk and sugar. Coffee is also used to make other drinks, such as café con leche, which is coffee with hot milk; café con hielo, which is coffee with ice; and café moka, which is coffee with chocolate and whipped cream. Coffee is also a symbol of the Costa Rican culture and identity, and it is often offered as a sign of hospitality and friendship.

**Agua Dulce**: Agua dulce, which means "sweet water" in Spanish, is a traditional hot drink that is made with tapa de dulce, which is a solid block of unrefined sugar cane. Tapa de dulce is dissolved in boiling water or milk, and sometimes flavored with cinnamon, vanilla, or ginger. Agua dulce is a simple and comforting drink that is usually consumed in the morning or at night, especially in rural areas or during the cold season. Agua dulce is also a nutritious and natural drink, as it provides energy and minerals.

**Coconut Water**: Coconut water is a refreshing and healthy drink that is extracted from young green coconuts. Coconut water is rich in electrolytes, vitamins, and antioxidants, and it has a sweet and slightly nutty taste. Coconut water is usually drunk straight from the coconut itself, with a straw or a spoon, and sometimes with a squeeze of lime juice. Coconut water is widely available in Costa Rica, especially on the Caribbean and Pacific coasts, where coconut palms are abundant. Coconut water is also used to make other drinks, such as coco loco, which is coconut water with rum and cream of coconut; and piña colada, which is coconut water with pineapple juice and rum.

**Natural Juices/Fruit Shakes:** Costa Rica is blessed with many tropical fruits that are delicious and nutritious, and they are often used to make natural juices or fruit shakes. Natural juices are made with fresh fruits, water, and ice, and sometimes sugar or honey. Fruit shakes are made with fresh fruits, milk, and ice, and sometimes yogurt or ice cream. Some of the most common fruits used to make juices or shakes are cas, which is a sour green fruit; mango, which is a sweet and juicy yellow fruit; pineapple, which is a sweet and tangy yellow fruit; blackberry, which is a tart and dark purple fruit; and soursop, which is a creamy and white fruit. Natural juices and fruit shakes are usually served cold, with or without a straw, and they are a great way to hydrate and nourish yourself.

## *Wine and Food Pairing*

Below are some tips and suggestions on how to pair wine and food in Costa Rica:

**Gallo pinto**: Gallo pinto is a hearty and savory dish that can pair well with a light and fruity white wine, such as a Chardonnay or a Sauvignon Blanc. These wines can balance the richness and spiciness of the dish, and complement the freshness and acidity of the salsa

Lizano.

**Casado**: Casado is a balanced and satisfying dish that can pair well with a medium-bodied and versatile red wine, such as a Merlot or a Pinot Noir. These wines can match the complexity and variety of the dish, and harmonize with the sweetness and starchiness of the plantains.

**Ceviche**: Ceviche is a refreshing and tangy dish that can pair well with a crisp and aromatic white wine, such as a Riesling or a Gewürztraminer. These wines can enhance the citrus and herbal flavors of the dish, and contrast with the spiciness and saltiness of the marinade.

**Olla de carne**: Olla de carne is a hearty and comforting dish that can pair well with a full-bodied and robust red wine, such as a Cabernet Sauvignon or a Malbec. These wines can stand up to the richness and meatiness of the dish, and accentuate the earthy and savory flavors of the broth.

**Sopa negra**: Sopa negra is a nutritious and delicious dish that can pair well with a smooth and fruity red wine, such as a Zinfandel or a Syrah. These wines can complement the nutty and smoky flavors of the beans, and add some sweetness and spice to the dish.

## *Must-Visit Costa Rican Restaurants*

Below are some of the must-visit Costa Rican restaurants that you should try while traveling in this beautiful country:

**La Criollita**: This is a well-known casual restaurant in San José that offers plates of classic Costa Rican dishes, such as gallo pinto, casado, olla de carne, and sopa negra. The portions are generous, the prices are reasonable, and the service is friendly. The restaurant is also decorated with traditional Costa Rican art and crafts, creating a cozy and authentic atmosphere. La Criollita is a great place to enjoy a hearty and savory breakfast, lunch, or dinner, and to experience the local flavors and culture of Costa Rica.

**Lizard King Café**: This is a laid-back morning café and restaurant located inside the Lizard King Resort in Puerto Viejo de Talamanca, a lively beach town on the Caribbean coast. The café offers a variety of dishes, such as pancakes, omelets, sandwiches, salads, and burgers, as well as fresh juices, smoothies, coffee, and tea. The café also has a vegan and gluten-free menu, catering to different dietary preferences. The café has a colorful and tropical décor, with a pool and a garden, creating a relaxing and fun vibe. Lizard King Café is a great place to enjoy a delicious and refreshing breakfast or brunch, and to mingle with other travelers and locals.

**Grano de Oro Restaurant**: This is a sophisticated restaurant that offers Costa Rican fusion cuisine in Hotel Grano de Oro, a luxury boutique hotel in San José. The restaurant uses fresh and local ingredients to create innovative and exquisite dishes, such as tuna tartare, lobster ravioli, lamb chops, and chocolate cake. The restaurant also has an extensive wine list, featuring wines from around the world. The restaurant has an elegant and romantic ambiance, with a courtyard, a fountain, and a fireplace, creating a memorable dining experience. Grano de Oro Restaurant is a great place to enjoy a fine and fancy dinner, and to celebrate a special occasion.

## *Culinary Experiences and Cooking Classes*

Below are some of the best culinary experiences and cooking classes that you can try while traveling in Costa Rica:

**Cooking and Salsa Dance Lesson Combo**: This is a

fun and interactive experience that combines learning to cook some traditional Costa Rican food with learning to dance some Latin dance styles, such as salsa, merengue, cumbia, and bachata. You will learn how to make dishes such as gallo pinto, casado, ceviche, and arroz con leche, using fresh and local ingredients. You will also learn how to move your hips and feet to the rhythm of the music, with the guidance of a professional instructor. You will enjoy a delicious meal and a lively dance party, and make some new friends along the way.

**Lizard King Café**: You can join one of the cooking classes that the café offers, where you will learn how to make some of the dishes on the menu, such as the banana pancakes, the veggie burger, or the coconut curry. You will also learn about the history and culture of the Caribbean coast, and the influence of the Afro-Caribbean cuisine on the Costa Rican cuisine.

**Grano de Oro Restaurant**: This is a sophisticated restaurant that offers Costa Rican fusion cuisine in Hotel Grano de Oro, a luxury boutique hotel in San José. The restaurant uses fresh and local ingredients to create innovative and exquisite dishes, such as tuna tartare, lobster ravioli, lamb chops, and chocolate cake. The restaurant also has an extensive wine list, featuring wines from around the world. The restaurant has an elegant and romantic ambiance, with a courtyard, a fountain, and a fireplace, creating a memorable dining experience. You can join one of the wine tasting sessions that the restaurant offers, where you will learn about the different types of wines, their origins, their characteristics, and their pairings with food. You will also taste some of the wines that the restaurant has to offer, and learn how to appreciate their flavors and aromas.

**Cooking Class Manuel Antonio:** This is a hands-on cooking class that takes place in a private home in Manuel Antonio, a popular tourist destination on the Pacific coast, known for its beaches, wildlife, and national park. You will learn how to make some of the lesser-known dishes that Costa Rica has to offer, such as tortillas, picadillo, tamales, and empanadas, using organic and seasonal ingredients from the garden. You will also learn how to cook in an open wood-fire kitchen, which is the traditional way of cooking in Costa Rica. You will enjoy a delicious and authentic meal, and learn about the Costa Rican culture and lifestyle from your host.

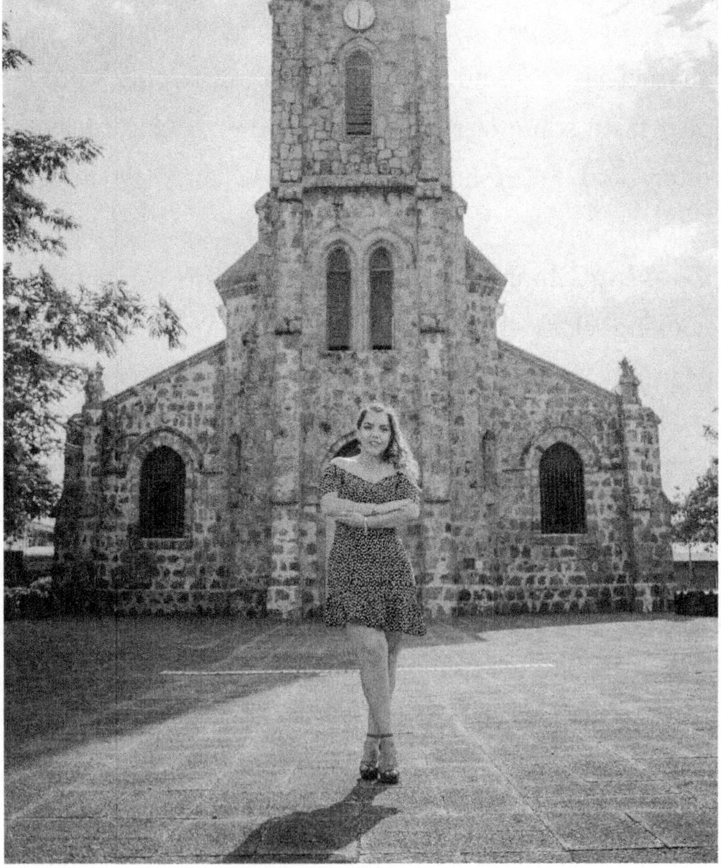

# Chapter 8 • Outdoor Activities and Entertainment

## *Canopy tours in Costa Rica*

One of the most exciting and adventurous ways to explore the natural beauty of Costa Rica is to take a canopy tour. A canopy tour is an activity that involves gliding through the treetops of the rainforest, the cloud forest, or the dry forest, using a system of cables, pulleys, and platforms. A canopy tour allows you to experience the forest from a different perspective, and to enjoy the stunning views of the landscape, the wildlife, and the vegetation.

There are many canopy tours in Costa Rica, each offering a unique and thrilling adventure. Depending on your preferences, budget, and location, you can find a canopy tour that suits your needs and expectations. Below are some of the best canopy tours in Costa Rica that you can book for your trip:

**Sky Trek:** This is one of the most popular and famous canopy tours in Costa Rica, and it is located in the

Arenal Volcano National Park, one of the most visited attractions in the country. Sky Trek consists of 10 zip lines, ranging from 200 to 750 meters in length, and reaching heights of up to 200 meters above the ground. You can enjoy the breathtaking views of the Arenal Volcano, the Arenal Lake, and the surrounding rainforest, as you fly through the air at speeds of up to 70 km/h. Sky Trek also offers an aerial tram, a hanging bridges walk, and a night tour, for a complete and unforgettable experience.

**Congo Trail Canopy Tour**: This is a fun and affordable canopy tour that is located in Guanacaste, a province known for its sunny and dry climate, and its beautiful beaches. Congo Trail Canopy Tour offers three different options: the original canopy tour, which has 11 zip lines and 14 platforms; the extreme canopy tour, which has 25 zip lines and 11 waterfalls; and the superman canopy tour, which has a 1.5 km long zip line that lets you fly like a superhero. You can also visit the monkey sanctuary, where you can interact with rescued monkeys, and the butterfly garden, where you can admire different species of butterflies.

**Sarapiqui River Sightseeing Cruise and Zipline Canopy Tour**: This is a combination of two activities that let you explore the Sarapiqui River and the rainforest that surrounds it. The Sarapiqui River is a scenic and biodiverse river that flows through the northern region of Costa Rica. You can take a sightseeing cruise along the river, and observe the wildlife that lives on its banks, such as crocodiles, monkeys, sloths, and birds. You can also take a zipline canopy tour, and glide through the treetops of the rainforest, and enjoy the views of the river and the mountains. This is a great way to experience the nature and the culture of Costa Rica.

## *Coffee tours in Costa Rica*

Costa Rica is famous for its high-quality coffee, which is grown in various regions with different climates, soils, and altitudes. If you are a coffee lover, you may want to take a coffee tour in Costa Rica, where you can learn about the history, culture, and production of this delicious beverage, and taste some of the best coffee in the world. Below are some of the best coffee tours in Costa Rica that you can choose from:

**Café Monteverde Coffee Tour**: This is a coffee tour that takes place in Monteverde, a cloud forest reserve that is home to many species of flora and fauna. You will learn about the history of the region and the coffee producers, and how the community developed as a result of coffee cultivation. You will also visit a coffee farm, where you will see the different stages of coffee production, from planting, harvesting, processing, roasting, and brewing. You will also taste some of the finest coffee in the country, and learn how to make your own café chorreado, the traditional Costa Rican way of preparing coffee. This tour lasts about 2 hours, and costs $35 per person.

**Doka Estate Coffee Tour:** This is a coffee tour that takes place in Doka Estate, a coffee plantation that is located on the slopes of the Poas Volcano, one of the most active volcanoes in the world. You will learn about the history of the estate and the coffee industry in Costa Rica, and how the volcanic soil and the altitude affect the quality and flavor of the coffee. You will also tour the facilities, where you will see the different processes of coffee production, such as wet milling, drying, sorting, roasting, and packaging. You will also taste some of the award-winning coffee that Doka Estate produces, and visit the coffee museum and the butterfly garden. This tour lasts about 3 hours, and costs $22 per person.

**Espiritu Santo Coffee Tour:** This is a coffee tour that

takes place in Espiritu Santo, a coffee cooperative that is located in Naranjo, a town in the Central Valley region. You will learn about the history of the cooperative and the coffee culture in Costa Rica, and how the cooperative supports the social and environmental development of the community. You will also visit a coffee farm, where you will see the different varieties of coffee plants, and how they are grown and harvested. You will also visit the roastery, where you will see how the coffee beans are roasted and ground, and how the different roasts affect the taste and aroma of the coffee. You will also taste some of the coffee that Espiritu Santo produces, and learn how to identify the different characteristics of coffee. This tour lasts about 2 hours, and costs $25 per person.

**The Classic Britt Coffee Tour**: This is a coffee tour that takes place in Britt, a coffee company that is located in Heredia, a city in the Central Valley region. You will learn about the history of the company and the coffee trade in Costa Rica, and how the company strives to produce high-quality and sustainable coffee. You will also tour the roastery, where you will see how the coffee beans are roasted and packaged, and how the company uses technology and innovation to improve the coffee quality and experience. You will also taste some of the coffee that Britt produces, and learn how to appreciate the different flavors and aromas of coffee. You will also visit the factory store, where you can buy some of the coffee, chocolates, cookies, and souvenirs that Britt offers. This tour lasts about 1.5 hours, and costs $22 per person.

# *Surfing and windsurfing in Costa Rica*

Below are some of the best surfing and windsurfing spots in Costa Rica that you can visit during your trip:

**Tamarindo Beach**: This is one of the most popular and accessible surfing spots in Costa Rica, located in the Guanacaste province on the Pacific coast. Tamarindo Beach has a wide range of waves, from gentle breaks for beginners to challenging barrels for experts. You can also find many surf shops, schools, and rentals in the town, as well as restaurants, bars, and hotels. Tamarindo Beach is also a good base to explore other nearby surfing spots, such as Playa Grande, Playa Langosta, and Playa Avellanas.

**Espadilla Beach**: This is a great surfing spot for beginners, located in the Manuel Antonio National Park on the Pacific coast. Espadilla Beach has a long and sandy beach, with soft and consistent waves that are ideal for learning and practicing. You can also enjoy the stunning scenery of the park, and the wildlife that inhabits it, such as monkeys, sloths, and birds. You can also find some surf shops, schools, and rentals in the area, as well as restaurants, cafes, and hotels.

**Jaco Beach**: This is a lively and convenient surfing spot, located in the Central Pacific coast. Jaco Beach has a long and wide beach, with waves that suit all levels of surfers, from beginners to pros. You can also find a variety of surf shops, schools, and rentals in the town, as well as nightlife, entertainment, and accommodation options. Jaco Beach is also close to other surfing spots, such as Hermosa Beach, Esterillos Beach, and Bejuco Beach.

**Lake Arenal**: This is the best windsurfing spot in Costa Rica, located in the Arenal Volcano National Park in the northern region. Lake Arenal is the largest lake in Costa Rica, and it has strong and steady winds that blow from December to April, creating ideal conditions for windsurfing. You can also enjoy the spectacular views of the Arenal Volcano, the lake, and the surrounding rainforest, as well as the activities and tours that the park offers, such as hiking, zip-lining, birdwatching, and more. You can also find some windsurfing shops, schools, and rentals in the area, as well as hotels, restaurants, and spas.

**Salinas Bay**: This is another excellent windsurfing spot in Costa Rica, located in the Guanacaste province on the Pacific coast. Salinas Bay is a remote and natural bay, with consistent and powerful winds that blow from November to May, creating perfect conditions for windsurfing and kite surfing. You can also enjoy the pristine and uncrowded beach, and the wildlife that lives in the area, such as turtles, dolphins, and whales. You can also find some windsurfing and kite surfing shops, schools, and rentals in the area, as well as hotels, restaurants, and bars.

## *Volcano watching in Costa Rica*

Volcano watching in Costa Rica is a thrilling and fascinating activity that allows you to witness the power and beauty of nature. Costa Rica has over 60 volcanoes, six of which are still active, and each one has its own unique features and attractions. Whether you want to see lava flows, geysers, hot springs, or crater lakes, you will find a volcano that suits your interests and expectations. Below are some of the best volcanoes to visit in Costa Rica for an unforgettable experience:

**Arenal Volcano**: This is the most iconic and famous volcano in Costa Rica, located in the northern region of the country. Arenal is a perfect cone-shaped volcano that erupted regularly until 2010, and now is dormant but still impressive. You can enjoy the stunning views of the volcano from various angles, and also explore the surrounding area, which offers many activities and tours, such as hiking, zip-lining, horseback riding, rafting, and more. You can also relax in the natural thermal hot springs that are heated by the volcano, and enjoy the spa treatments and the amenities of the resorts and hotels nearby.

**Poás Volcano**: This is one of the most accessible and popular volcanoes in Costa Rica, located in the Central Valley near the capital city of San José. Poás is one of the largest active volcanoes in the world, with two main craters that contain sulfuric lakes. The main crater is the largest and the most spectacular, with a diameter of 1.5 km and a depth of 300m. You can walk along the trails and the viewing platforms that lead to the edge of the crater, and admire the turquoise water and the steam that rise from the lake. You can also visit the other crater, called Botos, which has a cold and clear lake surrounded by the cloud forest. You can also explore the park and see the wildlife and the vegetation that live in the different habitats.

**Irazú Volcano:** This is the highest and the most impressive volcano in Costa Rica, located in the Central Valley near the city of Cartago. Irazú has four craters, one of which contains a green-tinted lake that contrasts with the gray and barren landscape. You can drive to the summit of the volcano, which is 3,432 m above sea level, and enjoy the panoramic views of the valley and the mountains. On a clear day, you can even see both the Pacific and the Atlantic oceans from the top of the volcano. You can also hike along the trails and the roads that connect the craters, and see the different geological formations and the vegetation that grow on the slopes of the volcano.

**Rincón de la Vieja Volcano:** This is the most adventurous and diverse volcano in Costa Rica, located in the Guanacaste province on the Pacific coast. Rincón de la Vieja is a complex volcano that has nine craters and two peaks, and is part of a national park that covers an area of 14,000 hectares. You can hike along the trails that lead to the active craters, where you can see the fumaroles, the mud pots, the geysers, and the hot springs that are created by the volcanic activity. You can also enjoy the scenery and the wildlife of the park, which include the dry forest, the wet forest, the waterfalls, the rivers, and the animals, such as monkeys, sloths, and birds. You can also join the activities and tours that the park offers, such as zip-lining, horseback riding, rafting, and more.

## *Nature cruise in Costa Rica*

Below are some of the best nature cruises in Costa Rica that you can book for your trip:

**Costa Rica & the Panama Canal**: This is an 8-day cruise that takes you from Puerto Caldera to Balboa, crossing the Panama Canal and visiting some of the most amazing destinations in Costa Rica and Panama. You will sail along the Pacific coast, stopping at Curu National Wildlife Refuge, Tortuga Island, Osa Peninsula, Golfo Dulce, Coiba National Park, and Granito de Oro Island. You will have the opportunity to see a variety of wildlife, such as monkeys, sloths, macaws, toucans, dolphins, whales, and turtles. You will also enjoy activities such as hiking, snorkeling, kayaking, and paddle boarding. You will also experience the engineering marvel of the Panama Canal, and learn about its history and significance. You will cruise on board the luxurious Silver Shadow, a 388-passenger vessel that offers spacious suites, fine dining, and personalized service.

**Wild Costa Rica Escape:** This is a 6-day cruise that takes you from Puerto Caldera to Puerto Caldera, exploring the wild and wonderful nature of Costa Rica. You will visit some of the most pristine and biodiverse places in the country, such as Manuel Antonio National Park, Corcovado National Park, Caño Island Biological Reserve, and Curu National Wildlife Refuge. You will have the chance to see some of the most iconic and endangered animals in Costa Rica, such as the scarlet macaw, the jaguar, the tapir, and the quetzal. You will also enjoy activities such as hiking, swimming, snorkeling, kayaking, and zodiac rides. You will cruise on board the National Geographic Quest, a 100-passenger expedition ship that offers comfortable cabins, a lounge, a library, a spa, and a fitness center.

**Coastal Adventures: Costa Rica & Panama**: This is an 8-day cruise that takes you from San Jose to Panama City, discovering the coastal wonders of Costa Rica and Panama. You will travel along the Caribbean coast, stopping at Tortuguero National Park, Bocas del Toro Archipelago, San Blas Islands, and Panama Canal. You will have the opportunity to see a variety of wildlife, such as crocodiles, turtles, frogs, hummingbirds, parrots, and monkeys. You will also enjoy activities such as rafting, surfing, fishing, diving, and sailing. You will also learn about the culture and history of the indigenous people, such as the Bribris, the Ngöbe-Buglé, and the Guna. You will cruise on board the Emerald Azzurra, a 100-passenger superyacht that offers stylish and spacious suites, a restaurant, a bar, a pool, and a wellness center.

## *Watersports in Costa Rica*

Below are some of the best water sports in Costa Rica that you should try while traveling in this beautiful country:

**Surfing**: Costa Rica is a surfer's paradise, with consistent waves, warm water, and stunning scenery. You can surf on both the Pacific and the Caribbean coasts, and find waves that range from gentle to challenging. Some of the most famous surfing spots in Costa Rica are Tamarindo Beach, Jaco Beach, Witch's Rock, Playa Grande, Playa Hermosa, and Salsa Brava.

You can also find many surf shops, schools, and rentals in the towns and villages along the coast, as well as restaurants, bars, and hotels. Surfing is a great way to experience the culture and the lifestyle of Costa Rica, and to have fun and adrenaline at the same time.

**Diving and Snorkeling**: Costa Rica is a diver's and snorkeler's dream, with rich and diverse marine life, coral reefs, caves, and shipwrecks. You can dive and snorkel on both the Pacific and the Caribbean coasts, and see a variety of fish, turtles, sharks, rays, dolphins, whales, and more. Some of the best diving and snorkeling spots in Costa Rica are Caño Island, Cocos Island, Catalina Island, Bat Islands, Manuel Antonio, and Cahuita. You can also find many dive shops, schools, and tours in the towns and villages along the coast, as well as equipment rentals and guides. Diving and snorkeling are great ways to explore the underwater world of Costa Rica, and to appreciate its beauty and biodiversity.

**Rafting and Kayaking**: Costa Rica is a rafter's and kayaker's adventure, with fast and furious rivers, rapids, and waterfalls. You can raft and kayak on various rivers in the country, and experience different levels of difficulty and excitement. Some of the best rafting and kayaking spots in Costa Rica are Pacuare River, Reventazon River, Sarapiqui River, Savegre River, and Corobici River. You can also find many rafting and kayaking shops, schools, and tours in the towns and villages near the rivers, as well as equipment rentals and guides. Rafting and kayaking are great ways to enjoy the nature and the scenery of Costa Rica, and to have a thrilling and memorable experience.

**Fishing**: Costa Rica is a fisher's delight, with abundant and varied fish, both in freshwater and saltwater. You can fish on both the Pacific and the Caribbean coasts, and catch fish such as tuna, sailfish, marlin, mahi-mahi, roosterfish, and more. You can also fish on the lakes and rivers in the country, and catch fish such as bass, trout, tilapia, and more. You can join one of the many fishing tours, charters, or lodges in the country, or rent your own boat and equipment. Fishing is a great way to relax and have fun in Costa Rica, and to enjoy the fresh and delicious seafood.

## *Beaches and Coastal Experiences*

Below are some of the best beaches and coastal experiences that you can enjoy in Costa Rica:

**Manuel Antonio Beach**: This is one of the most popular and beautiful beaches in Costa Rica, located in the Manuel Antonio National Park on the Pacific coast. Manuel Antonio Beach is a white sand beach that is surrounded by lush rainforest and wildlife, such as monkeys, sloths, and birds. You can swim, sunbathe, or snorkel in the clear and calm water, or hike in the park and see the other beaches and attractions. You can also find many hotels, restaurants, and shops nearby, as well as tours and activities, such as kayaking, fishing, and sailing.

**Tamarindo Beach**: This is one of the most lively and fun beaches in Costa Rica, located in the Guanacaste province on the Pacific coast. Tamarindo Beach is a long and wide beach that has consistent waves and warm water, making it ideal for surfing, especially for beginners. You can also find many surf shops, schools, and rentals in the town, as well as nightlife, entertainment, and accommodation options. Tamarindo Beach is also a good base to explore other nearby beaches and attractions, such as Playa Grande, Playa Langosta, and Playa Avellanas.

**Tortuguero National Park**: This is one of the most unique and amazing coastal experiences in Costa Rica, located on the Caribbean coast. Tortuguero National Park is a remote and natural paradise that is famous for its canals, wildlife, and turtle nesting. You can take a boat or a kayak tour along the canals, and observe the animals that live in the water and on the land, such as crocodiles, monkeys, sloths, and birds. You can also visit the beach at night, and see the sea turtles laying their eggs, or the baby turtles hatching and making their way to the sea. You can also find some hotels, lodges, and tours in the area, as well as a turtle museum and a village.

**Caño Island**: This is one of the best diving and snorkeling spots in Costa Rica, located off the Osa Peninsula on the Pacific coast. Caño Island is a marine reserve that has a rich and diverse coral reef, and a variety of fish and marine animals, such as sharks, rays, dolphins, whales, and turtles. You can take a boat tour from Drake Bay or Sierpe, and enjoy the underwater scenery and the wildlife. You can also visit the island itself, and see the archaeological sites and the trails that lead to the viewpoints.

# *Nature walk in Costa Rica*

Below are some of the best nature walks in Costa Rica

that you can try while traveling in this beautiful country:

**Rio Celeste Waterfall Hike**: This is a moderate hike that takes you to one of the most stunning natural attractions in Costa Rica, the Rio Celeste Waterfall. The Rio Celeste is a river that has a unique turquoise color, due to a chemical reaction between the minerals in the water. The hike starts at the Tenorio Volcano National Park, and follows a trail through the rainforest, where you can see various plants and animals, such as bromeliads, orchids, monkeys, and birds. The hike ends at the waterfall, where you can admire the contrast between the blue water and the green vegetation, and take some amazing photos. The hike is about 7 km (4.3 mi) long, and takes about 4 hours to complete.

**Sendero Bosque Nuboso Trail**: This is an easy hike that takes you through the Monteverde Cloud Forest Reserve, one of the most biodiverse and pristine places in Costa Rica. The cloud forest is a type of rainforest that is covered by mist and clouds, creating a humid and cool environment. The hike follows a loop trail that passes by different habitats, such as the lower montane forest, the oak forest, and the elfin forest. You can see a variety of plants and animals, such as ferns, mosses, epiphytes, hummingbirds, quetzals, and coatis. The hike is about

3.6 km (2.2 mi) long, and takes about 2 hours to complete.

**Cerro Chirripó Grande:** This is a challenging hike that takes you to the highest peak in Costa Rica, the Cerro Chirripó Grande. The peak is 3,820m (12,533 ft) above sea level, and offers spectacular views of the country and the surrounding mountains. The hike starts at the town of San Gerardo de Rivas, and follows a steep and rocky trail that ascends through different ecosystems, such as the tropical forest, the cloud forest, the paramo, and the alpine tundra. You can see a variety of plants and animals, such as oaks, bamboo, bromeliads, tapirs, deer, and condors. The hike is about 20 km (12.4 mi) long, and takes about 10 hours to complete. You need to book a permit and a reservation at the base camp in advance, and be prepared for cold and windy weather at the summit.

## *Wellness: Spas, Retreats, and Yoga*

Below are some of the best wellness options in Costa Rica that you can consider for your trip:

**Spas**: Costa Rica has many spas that offer a variety of treatments and services, such as massages, facials, body wraps, aromatherapy, and more. You can find spas in different settings, such as hotels, resorts, or standalone facilities, and in different locations, such as the beach, the mountain, or the city. Some of the best spas in Costa Rica are Vida Mía Healing Center and Spa, which is part of The Retreat Costa Rica, a luxury wellness resort and spa located in a rainforest and a crystal quartz mountain; Tabacón Thermal Resort & Spa, which is a five-star resort and spa that features natural hot springs, waterfalls, and gardens, heated by the Arenal Volcano; and Harmony Hotel, which is a boutique hotel and spa that offers holistic and sustainable wellness services, such as yoga, meditation, acupuncture, and herbal medicine.

**Retreats**: Costa Rica has many retreats that offer a variety of programs and experiences, such as detox, healing, weight loss, spiritual, and more. You can find retreats in different settings, such as eco-lodges, farms, or villas, and in different locations, such as the jungle, the beach, or the valley. Some of the best retreats in Costa Rica are Pura Vida Retreat & Spa, which is a wellness and yoga retreat that offers customized packages, such as yoga, meditation, spa, adventure, and more; Rythmia Life Advancement Center, which is a transformational and spiritual retreat that offers ayahuasca ceremonies, plant medicine, breathwork, and metaphysical teachings; and Blue Osa Yoga Retreat & Spa, which is a secluded and serene retreat that offers yoga, spa, farm-to-table meals, and volunteer opportunities.

**Yoga**: Costa Rica is a yoga lover's paradise, with many yoga centers, studios, and teachers that offer a variety of styles, levels, and classes. You can practice yoga in different settings, such as the beach, the forest, or the mountain, and enjoy the views, the sounds, and the vibes of nature. You can also join one of the many yoga retreats that are available in Costa Rica, where you can deepen your practice, learn from experts, and meet like-minded people. Some of the best yoga centers and retreats in Costa Rica are Montezuma Yoga, which is a yoga center that offers daily classes, workshops, and retreats in a beautiful and peaceful setting overlooking the ocean; The Sanctuary at Two Rivers, which is a yoga retreat that offers luxury accommodations, gourmet vegetarian meals, and yoga classes in a private and exclusive tropical paradise; and Anamaya Resort, which is a yoga resort that offers stunning accommodations, organic meals, yoga classes, and circus entertainment in a breathtaking location near the Montezuma waterfalls.

# Chapter 9 • Shopping in Costa Rica

## *Fashion and Luxury Shopping*

Below are some of the best places to indulge in fashion and luxury shopping in Costa Rica:

**Multiplaza Escazú**: This is the largest and most upscale shopping mall in Costa Rica, located in the affluent suburb of Escazú, about 9 km from downtown San José. Multiplaza Escazú has over 350 stores, including international brands such as Armani, Burberry, Chanel, Gucci, Prada, and Tiffany & Co. You can also find local and regional brands, such as Britt Shop, Simán, and Arturo Calle. The mall also has a variety of restaurants, cafes, bars, and entertainment options, such as a cinema, a casino, and a bowling alley. Multiplaza Escazú is a great place to enjoy a day of shopping, dining, and fun in a modern and elegant setting.

**Avenida Escazú**: This is a trendy and chic shopping and lifestyle center, located next to Multiplaza Escazú. Avenida Escazú has a mix of stores, restaurants, hotels, offices, and residences, creating a vibrant and cosmopolitan atmosphere. You can find some of the most exclusive and fashionable stores in Costa Rica, such as Max Mara, Carolina Herrera, Hugo Boss, and Salvatore Ferragamo. You can also find some of the best art galleries, such as Galería Valanti, Galería Andrómeda, and Galería Nacional. Avenida Escazú also hosts events and festivals, such as fashion shows, concerts, and art exhibitions, making it a cultural and social hotspot in Costa Rica.

**Lincoln Plaza**: This is a modern and sophisticated shopping mall, located in the district of Moravia, about 5 km from downtown San José. Lincoln Plaza has over 200 stores, including international brands such as Zara, Mango, Lacoste, and Swarovski. You can also find local and regional brands, such as Cemaco, Universal, and Arenas. The mall also has a variety of restaurants, cafes, and entertainment options, such as a cinema, a theater, and a children's playground. Lincoln Plaza is a great place to shop, eat, and have fun in a stylish and comfortable setting.

## *Local Markets and Souvenirs*

Below are some of the best local markets and souvenirs that you can visit and buy in Costa Rica:

**Artesenal Market**: This is the largest and most famous souvenir market in Costa Rica, located in downtown San José. The market has over 90 stalls that sell a wide range of products, such as wood carvings, leather goods, ceramics, jewelry, paintings, and textiles. You can find some of the most authentic and unique souvenirs from Costa Rica, such as chorreadors (traditional coffee makers), ocarinas (clay flutes), and painted ox carts. The market is open every day from 8 am to 6 pm, and you can bargain with the vendors to get the best prices.

**Central Market**: This is the oldest and most traditional market in Costa Rica, located in downtown San José. The market has over 200 shops that sell a variety of products, such as fruits, vegetables, meat, cheese, spices, herbs, flowers, and more. You can also find some of the best food and drinks in Costa Rica, such as gallo pinto (rice and beans), casado (mixed plate), ceviche (raw fish marinated in citrus juice), and agua dulce (sugar cane drink). The market is open every day from 6 am to 6 pm, and you can experience the culture and the lifestyle of Costa Rica.

**Souvenir Museum**: This is a unique and innovative souvenir shop and museum, located in Alajuela, about

20 km from San José. The shop and museum sell and display a variety of products that are made by local artisans and artists, using recycled and natural materials, such as paper, glass, metal, wood, and fabric. You can find some of the most creative and eco-friendly souvenirs from Costa Rica, such as jewelry, bags, notebooks, lamps, and sculptures. The shop and museum are open from Monday to Saturday from 9 am to 5 pm, and you can also take a tour and learn about the history and the process of making the products.

## *Artisan Crafts and Workshops*

Below are some of the best artisan crafts and workshops that you can enjoy in Costa Rica:

**Wood Carving**: Wood carving is one of the most common and popular crafts in Costa Rica, and it reflects the country's natural and agricultural heritage. You can find wood carvings of different shapes, sizes, and themes, such as animals, plants, masks, religious figures, and musical instruments. You can also find the famous painted ox carts, which are colorful and intricate representations of the rural life and the history of Costa Rica. You can buy wood carvings from various markets and shops, such as the Artesenal Market and the Crafts

& Artisans Market in San José, or the Souvenir Museum in Alajuela. You can also join a wood carving workshop, such as the one offered by the Sarchi artisan town, which is the cradle of Costa Rican handicrafts and the home of the largest ox cart in the world.

**Ceramics**: Ceramics is another craft that is widely practiced and appreciated in Costa Rica, and it reflects the country's indigenous and colonial influences. You can find ceramics of different styles, colors, and designs, such as pots, plates, bowls, vases, and figurines. You can also find the unique ocarinas, which are clay flutes that produce different sounds depending on the shape and the holes. You can buy ceramics from various markets and shops, such as the Central Market and the Souvenir Museum in San José, or the Crafts & Artisans Market in Alajuela. You can also join a ceramics workshop, such as the one offered by the Guaitil pottery village, which is a community of Chorotega indigenous people who preserve and share their ancestral techniques and traditions of making ceramics.

**Textiles**: Textiles is another craft that is widely practiced and appreciated in Costa Rica, and it reflects the country's tropical and colorful culture. You can find textiles of different materials, patterns, and uses, such as cotton, wool, silk, batik, tie-dye, and embroidery. You can also find textiles that are used for clothing, accessories, bags, hammocks, and home décor. You can buy textiles from various markets and shops, such as the Artesenal Market and the Central Market in San José, or the Souvenir Museum in Alajuela. You can also join a textiles workshop, such as the one offered by the Boruca indigenous reserve, which is a community of Brunka indigenous people who create and sell their distinctive and symbolic masks and textiles.

## *Antique and Vintage Shopping*

Below are some of the best places to go antique and vintage shopping in Costa Rica:

**Central Market (Mercado Central):** This is the largest and oldest market in San Jose, the capital city of Costa Rica. It was founded in 1880 and covers an area of 6,500 square meters. It has more than 200 stalls and shops that sell everything from fresh produce, meat, cheese, and coffee, to clothes, hats, cigars, and souvenirs. You can also find some antique and vintage items, such as old coins, stamps, postcards, maps, and magazines. The market is also a great place to sample the local cuisine, as there are many small cafes and restaurants that serve traditional dishes, such as gallo pinto, casado, and chifrijo. The market is open every day from 6:30 a.m. to 6:00 p.m.

**National Craft Market (Mercado Nacional de Artesania):** This is a one-stop-shop for souvenir shopping in Costa Rica, where you can find handcrafted items made by local artisans. The market is located near the Central Park in San Jose, and it offers a wide range of products, such as pottery, woodcarving, leather, textiles, jewelry, and paintings. You can also find some antique and vintage items, such as masks, dolls, musical instruments, and religious icons. The market is open every day from 9:00 a.m. to 5:00 p.m.

**Eco Market El Coco**: This is a weekly market that takes place every Saturday from 8:00 a.m. to 1:00 p.m. in the town of El Coco, in the province of Guanacaste. The market is dedicated to promoting organic and sustainable products, such as fruits, vegetables, honey, cheese, bread, and coffee. You can also find some antique and vintage items, such as books, records, clothing, and accessories. The market is a great place to meet the local producers and artisans, and to enjoy the live music and entertainment.

**Old Harbor Art & Craft Market**: This is a monthly

market that takes place every first Sunday of the month from 10:00 a.m. to 4:00 p.m. in the town of Puerto Viejo, in the province of Limon. The market is located in the old harbor, next to the beach, and it showcases the work of local artists and crafters. You can find a variety of products, such as paintings, sculptures, jewelry, clothing, and bags. You can also find some antique and vintage items, such as cameras, radios, typewriters, and bicycles. The market is a fun and colorful event, where you can also enjoy the Caribbean vibe and culture.

**Tamarindo Night Market**: This is a seasonal market that takes place every Thursday from 6:00 p.m. to 10:00 p.m. in the town of Tamarindo, in the province of Guanacaste. The market is located in the parking lot of the Garden Plaza, and it features more than 40 vendors that sell a variety of products, such as food, drinks, clothing, jewelry, and art. You can also find some antique and vintage items, such as lamps, mirrors, frames, and posters. The market is a lively and festive event, where you can also enjoy the live music and performances.

# Chapter 10 • Practical Information

## *Health and Safety Tips*

Below are some tips to help you stay healthy and safe during your trip to Costa Rica:

**Before you go**: Visit your doctor at least a month before your trip to get any vaccines or medicines you may need. Some of the recommended vaccines for Costa Rica are COVID-19, hepatitis A, hepatitis B, malaria, measles, and rabies. You should also check the travel health notices for Costa Rica to see if there are any outbreaks or advisories. Make sure you have a valid passport, travel insurance, and emergency contacts. Pack a first aid kit, insect repellent, sunscreen, and any prescription or over-the-counter medications you may need.

**While you are there**: Eat and drink safely. Avoid tap water, ice, and unpasteurized dairy products. Drink bottled or filtered water, or boil it for at least one minute before drinking. Eat only cooked or peeled fruits and vegetables, and avoid street food or food from vendors without proper hygiene. Wash your hands often with soap and water, or use alcohol-based hand sanitizer.

**Prevent bug bites**. Bugs (like mosquitoes, ticks, and fleas) can spread a number of diseases in Costa Rica, such as dengue, Zika, chikungunya, and yellow fever. Use insect repellent that contains DEET, picaridin, or oil of lemon eucalyptus. Wear long-sleeved shirts, long pants, and socks, and tuck your pants into your socks. Sleep under a mosquito net or in an air-conditioned room with screens on the windows and doors.

**Stay safe outdoors**. Costa Rica has many natural attractions, such as volcanoes, rainforests, beaches, and wildlife. However, these also pose some hazards, such as landslides, floods, earthquakes, venomous animals, and rabies. Follow the local authorities' instructions and warnings, and do not enter restricted areas. Wear appropriate clothing and footwear, and use protective equipment when engaging in outdoor activities, such as hiking, biking, rafting, or zip-lining. Do not touch or feed wild animals, and keep a safe distance from them. If you are bitten or scratched by an animal, wash the wound with soap and water, and seek medical attention immediately.

**Keep away from crime**. Costa Rica is generally a safe country, but petty crimes, such as theft, robbery, and pickpocketing, are common, especially in urban areas and tourist spots. Avoid isolated areas, especially at night, and stay where there are people around. Do not wear flashy items or display expensive jewelry to avoid attracting unnecessary attention. Keep your belongings secure at all times and avoid leaving them unattended, particularly on beaches or in public areas. Use only licensed taxis or reputable transportation services, and do not accept rides from strangers. Be aware of your surroundings and trust your instincts.

**In case of emergency**: Dial 911 for emergency assistance. The Red Cross Rescue unit may be reached directly at 128 throughout the country (2221-5818 in San José). Tourism Care Medical Services has road and air paramedic and ambulance service throughout Costa Rica (2286-1818). You can also contact your embassy or consulate for help.

## *Emergency Contacts*

Below are some of the emergency contacts in Costa Rica that you should have handy during your trip:

**911**: This is the main emergency number in Costa Rica, and it covers the following services: police, fire, ambulance, national emergency commission, national intoxication center, civil guard, judicial investigation bureau, and others. You can dial this number from any phone, and there are operators who can speak English to assist you. This number should be used for any urgent or life-threatening situation, such as accidents, crimes, fires, medical emergencies, natural disasters, or poisonings.

**128**: This is the alternative number for ambulance service in Costa Rica, and it connects you to the local Red Cross, which provides prompt medical assistance and transportation to the nearest hospital. You can use this number if you need an ambulance but the situation is not critical or if you cannot reach 911.

**118**: This is the alternative number for fire service in Costa Rica, and it connects you to the local fire fighters, who can respond to any fire-related emergency. You can use this number if you need to report a fire but the situation is not urgent or if you cannot reach 911.

**2221-5337 or 2222-1365**: These are the numbers for the Judicial Investigation Bureau (OIJ), which is the organization in charge of conducting criminal investigations in Costa Rica. You can use these numbers if you need to report a crime, such as theft, robbery, assault, or fraud, or if you are a victim or witness of a crime. You can also contact the OIJ if you need to file a police report for insurance purposes.

**2222-9330 or 800-8726-7486**: These are the numbers for the Transit Police, which manage all car traffic affairs and should be contacted for highway emergencies, such as car accidents, breakdowns, or traffic violations. You can use these numbers if you need assistance on the road or if you are involved in a traffic incident.

**+506 2519-2000**: This is the number for the United States Embassy in Costa Rica, and it can be used for any consular assistance, such as passport, visa, or citizenship issues, or if you need help in case of an emergency. You can also contact the embassy if you lose your passport or if it is stolen or damaged. The embassy is located in San Jose, the capital city of Costa Rica, and it is open from Monday to Friday, from 8:00 a.m. to 4:30 p.m.

## *Communication and Internet Access*

Below are some of the options and tips for communication and internet access in Costa Rica:

**Phone**: Costa Rica has a well-developed phone network that covers most of the country. The country code is

+506, and there are no area codes. To make a local call, you just need to dial the eight-digit number. To make an international call, you need to dial 00 followed by the country code and the phone number. You can use public payphones, which accept coins or prepaid cards, to make local or international calls. You can also use your own mobile phone, if it is compatible with the local network and unlocked. Costa Rica has three main mobile operators: Kolbi, Claro, and Movistar. They offer prepaid SIM cards that you can buy at their offices, kiosks, or convenience stores. You can also buy airtime credit at these locations or online. The prepaid SIM cards usually include data, voice, and text services, and they are valid for 30 days. The rates vary depending on the operator and the plan, but they are generally affordable and convenient.

**Internet**: Costa Rica has a high internet penetration rate, with more than 80% of the population. The country offers various types of internet services, including wireless, broadband, and high-speed internet. Wireless internet is widely available in Costa Rica, with many public places such as cafes, hotels, and restaurants offering free Wi-Fi to their customers. However, the reliability and speed of Wi-Fi networks can vary greatly, especially in rural areas where connectivity may be limited. Broadband internet is generally considered to be the more reliable and faster option for internet access in Costa Rica. The broadband market is dominated by a few major internet service providers, such as ICE, Tigo, and Movistar. These providers offer various broadband technologies such as fiber optic, DSL, and cable to meet different needs and budgets. You can subscribe to a broadband internet plan at their offices or online, or you can use their prepaid internet services, which allow you to pay for the amount of data or time you use. High-speed internet is also available in Costa Rica, with some providers offering speeds of up to 300 Mbps. However, this option is more expensive and less accessible, as it requires a fiber optic connection and a compatible device.

**Tips**: Below are some tips to help you communicate and access the internet in Costa Rica:

Check your phone compatibility and roaming charges before traveling to Costa Rica. If your phone is not compatible or the roaming charges are too high, you can buy a local SIM card or rent a phone in Costa Rica.

Use online communication apps, such as WhatsApp, Skype, or Zoom, to make free or low-cost calls and messages over the internet. You can also use these apps to stay in touch with your family and friends back home. Use a VPN (virtual private network) to protect your online privacy and security, especially when using public Wi-Fi networks. A VPN encrypts your data and allows you to access geo-restricted websites and content.

# Chapter 11 • Recommended Itineraries

## *One Day in Costa Rica*

Below are some suggestions for how to spend one day in Costa Rica, depending on your preferences and interests:

If you love nature and wildlife, you can visit one of the many national parks and reserves that Costa Rica has to offer. For example, you can go to Manuel Antonio National Park, which is considered one of the most beautiful parks in Costa Rica. On this tour, you will enjoy a scenic drive along the Pacific coast, and then explore the park with a guide who will show you the diverse flora and fauna, such as monkeys, sloths, iguanas, and birds. You will also have some free time to relax on the white-sand beaches or swim in the turquoise waters. Another option is to visit the Poas Volcano National Park, where you can admire the impressive crater of one of the most active volcanoes in the world. You can also visit the Doka Coffee Estate, where you can learn about the coffee production process and taste some of the best coffee in the world. You can also visit the La Paz Waterfall Gardens, where you can see stunning waterfalls, butterflies, hummingbirds, and orchids.

If you love adventure and adrenaline, you can choose one of the many outdoor activities that Costa Rica offers, such as zip-lining, rafting, hiking, or biking. For example, you can go to the Arenal Volcano area, where you can enjoy a thrilling zip-line tour over the rainforest canopy, with views of the majestic volcano and the lake. You can also visit the La Fortuna Waterfall, where you can take a refreshing dip in the natural pool, or the Arenal Hot Springs, where you can relax in the mineral-rich waters. Another option is to go to the Sarapiqui River, where you can experience a fun and exciting rafting adventure on the rapids, surrounded by lush vegetation and wildlife. You can also visit a local farm, where you can learn about the rural life and culture of Costa Rica.

If you love culture and history, you can explore the capital city of San Jose, where you can discover the rich Costa Rican heritage and traditions. You can visit some of the museums, such as the National Museum, where you can see exhibits of pre-Columbian art, colonial history, and natural history, or the Gold Museum, where you can see a collection of gold artifacts from different indigenous cultures. You can also visit some of the historical buildings, such as the National Theater, which is a neoclassical masterpiece, or the Metropolitan Cathedral, which is a blend of different architectural styles. You can also enjoy some of the cultural activities, such as watching a performance, listening to live music, or tasting some of the local cuisine.

## *Three Days in Costa Rica*

If you have three days to spend in this beautiful country, below is a suggested itinerary that will allow you to experience some of the best attractions and activities that Costa Rica has to offer:

**Day 1:** San Jose and Poas Volcano. Start your trip by exploring the capital city of San Jose, where you can visit some of the mutrseums, such as the National Museum or the Gold Museum, and admire some of the historical buildings, such as the National Theater or the Metropolitan Cathedral. In the afternoon, take a scenic drive to the Poas Volcano National Park, where you can see the impressive crater of one of the most active volcanoes in the world. You can also visit the Doka Coffee Estate, where you can learn about the coffee production process and taste some of the best coffee in the world.

**Day 2**: Arenal Volcano and La Fortuna. Head to the Arenal Volcano area, where you can enjoy a thrilling zip-line tour over the rainforest canopy, with views of the majestic volcano and the lake. You can also visit the La Fortuna Waterfall, where you can take a refreshing dip in the natural pool, or the Arenal Hot Springs, where you can relax in the mineral-rich waters. In the evening, you can enjoy some of the nightlife and entertainment options in the town of La Fortuna.

**Day 3**: Manuel Antonio National Park. Drive to the Pacific coast, where you can visit the Manuel Antonio National Park, which is considered one of the most beautiful parks in Costa Rica. On this tour, you will explore the park with a guide who will show you the diverse flora and fauna, such as monkeys, sloths, iguanas, and birds. You will also have some free time to relax on the white-sand beaches or swim in the turquoise waters. You can also enjoy some of the water sports and activities, such as surfing, kayaking, or snorkeling.

## *Five Days in Costa Rica*

If you have five days to spend in this beautiful country, below is a suggested itinerary that will allow you to experience some of the best attractions and activities that Costa Rica has to offer:

**Day 1:** San Jose and Poas Volcano. Start your trip by exploring the capital city of San Jose, where you can visit some of the museums, such as the National Museum or the Gold Museum, and admire some of the historical buildings, such as the National Theater or the Metropolitan Cathedral. In the afternoon, take a scenic drive to the Poas Volcano National Park, where you can see the impressive crater of one of the most active volcanoes in the world. You can also visit the Doka Coffee Estate, where you can learn about the coffee production process and taste some of the best coffee in the world.

**Day 2:** Arenal Volcano and La Fortuna. Head to the Arenal Volcano area, where you can enjoy a thrilling zip-line tour over the rainforest canopy, with views of the majestic volcano and the lake. You can also visit the La Fortuna Waterfall, where you can take a refreshing dip in the natural pool, or the Arenal Hot Springs, where you can relax in the mineral-rich waters. In the evening, you can enjoy some of the nightlife and entertainment options in the town of La Fortuna.

**Day 3:** Monteverde Cloud Forest. Drive to the Monteverde Cloud Forest, where you can experience one of the most biodiverse and unique ecosystems in the world. On this tour, you will walk along the hanging bridges and trails that offer stunning views of the forest and its wildlife. You can also visit the hummingbird garden, where you can see dozens of these colorful and fast birds, or the butterfly garden, where you can admire hundreds of different species of butterflies. You can also enjoy some of the adventure activities, such as bungee jumping, horseback riding, or ATV tours.

**Day 4:** Manuel Antonio National Park. Drive to the Pacific coast, where you can visit the Manuel Antonio National Park, which is considered one of the most beautiful parks in Costa Rica. On this tour, you will explore the park with a guide who will show you the diverse flora and fauna, such as monkeys, sloths, iguanas, and birds. You will also have some free time to relax on the white-sand beaches or swim in the turquoise waters. You can also enjoy some of the water sports and activities, such as surfing, kayaking, or snorkeling.

**Day 5:** Tortuguero National Park. Take a flight or a boat ride to the Caribbean coast, where you can visit the Tortuguero National Park, which is famous for its sea turtle nesting and hatching. On this tour, you will take a boat ride along the canals and lagoons that are home to a variety of wildlife, such as crocodiles, caimans, otters, and manatees. You will also visit the turtle museum, where you can learn about the life cycle and conservation of these amazing creatures. If you are lucky, you may even witness the nesting or hatching of the turtles, depending on the season.

## *Seven Days in Costa Rica*

If you have seven days to spend in this beautiful country, below is a suggested itinerary that will allow you to experience some of the best attractions and activities that Costa Rica has to offer:

**Day 1:** San Jose and Poas Volcano. Start your trip by exploring the capital city of San Jose, where you can visit some of the museums, such as the National Museum or the Gold Museum, and admire some of the historical buildings, such as the National Theater or the Metropolitan Cathedral. In the afternoon, take a scenic drive to the Poas Volcano National Park, where you can see the impressive crater of one of the most active volcanoes in the world. You can also visit the Doka Coffee Estate, where you can learn about the coffee production process and taste some of the best coffee in the world.

**Day 2:** Arenal Volcano and La Fortuna. Head to the Arenal Volcano area, where you can enjoy a thrilling zip-line tour over the rainforest canopy, with views of the majestic volcano and the lake. You can also visit the La Fortuna Waterfall, where you can take a refreshing dip in the natural pool, or the Arenal Hot Springs, where you can relax in the mineral-rich waters. In the evening, you can enjoy some of the nightlife and entertainment options in the town of La Fortuna.

**Day 3:** Monteverde Cloud Forest. Drive to the Monteverde Cloud Forest, where you can experience one of the most biodiverse and unique ecosystems in the world. On this tour, you will walk along the hanging bridges and trails that offer stunning views of the forest and its wildlife. You can also visit the hummingbird garden, where you can see dozens of these colorful and fast birds, or the butterfly garden, where you can admire hundreds of different species of butterflies. You can also enjoy some of the adventure activities, such as bungee jumping, horseback riding, or ATV tours.

**Day 4:** Manuel Antonio National Park. Drive to the Pacific coast, where you can visit the Manuel Antonio National Park, which is considered one of the most beautiful parks in Costa Rica. On this tour, you will explore the park with a guide who will show you the diverse flora and fauna, such as monkeys, sloths, iguanas, and birds. You will also have some free time to relax on the white-sand beaches or swim in the turquoise waters. You can also enjoy some of the water sports and activities, such as surfing, kayaking, or snorkeling.

**Day 5:** Tortuguero National Park. Take a flight or a boat ride to the Caribbean coast, where you can visit the Tortuguero National Park, which is famous for its sea turtle nesting and hatching. On this tour, you will take a boat ride along the canals and lagoons that are home to a variety of wildlife, such as crocodiles, caimans, otters, and manatees. You will also visit the turtle museum, where you can learn about the life cycle and conservation of these amazing creatures. If you are lucky, you may even witness the nesting or hatching of the turtles, depending on the season.

**Day 6:** Corcovado National Park. Take another flight or a boat ride to the Osa Peninsula, where you can visit the Corcovado National Park, which is considered one of the most biologically intense places on earth. On this tour, you will hike through the pristine rainforest, where you can see some of the rarest and most endangered animals in the world, such as jaguars, tapirs, macaws, and anteaters. You will also have some free time to enjoy the secluded beaches or the marine life, such as dolphins, whales, and turtles.

**Day 7:** San Jose. Return to San Jose, where you can do some last-minute shopping, sightseeing, or relaxing. You can also visit some of the cultural attractions, such as the Pre-Columbian Jade Museum, where you can see a collection of jade artifacts from different indigenous cultures, or the National Theater, where you can watch a performance, listen to live music, or taste some of the local cuisine.

# Chapter 12 • Travelling with Children

## *Child-Friendly Attractions*

Below are some of the best child-friendly attractions in Costa Rica:

**Tortuga Island Tour:** This is a full-day tour that takes you to the beautiful Tortuga Island, located in the Gulf of Nicoya. You will enjoy a catamaran cruise that will let you see dolphins, whales, and other marine life along the way. Once you arrive at the island, you can relax on the white-sand beach, swim in the crystal-clear water, or join some of the water activities, such as snorkeling, kayaking, or banana boat. You will also have a delicious lunch and live music on board. This tour is suitable for children of all ages, and it will give you a tropical paradise experience.

**Manuel Antonio National Park**: This is one of the most popular and biodiverse national parks in Costa Rica, where you can see a variety of animals, such as monkeys, sloths, iguanas, and birds. You can join a guided tour that will show you the best spots to observe and learn about the wildlife, or you can explore the park on your own. You will also have some free time to enjoy the stunning beaches and the warm ocean. This tour is suitable for children of 4 years and older, and it will give you a nature and wildlife adventure.

**Surf Lesson in Tamarindo**: This is a fun and exciting activity that will teach you how to surf in one of the best surfing spots in Costa Rica. You will have a professional instructor who will guide you step by step, from the basics to the advanced techniques. You will also have all the equipment and safety measures provided. You can choose from different options, such as private, semi-private, or group lessons, depending on your preference and budget. This activity is suitable for children of 4 years and older, and it will give you a surfing challenge and thrill.

**Diamante Eco Adventure Park:** This is a family-friendly attraction that offers a variety of activities, such as zip-lining, animal sanctuary, botanical garden, and cultural experience. You can choose from different packages, such as the adventure pass, the discovery pass, or the combo pass, depending on your interest and time. You will be able to fly over the rainforest canopy, see exotic animals, such as jaguars, monkeys, and sloths, learn about the plants and herbs, and taste some of the local cuisine. This attraction is suitable for children of 5 years and older, and it will give you a fun and educational experience.

**La Fortuna Waterfall**: This is a spectacular waterfall that is located near the town of La Fortuna, in the Arenal Volcano area. You can access the waterfall by hiking down a trail that takes about 20 minutes, or by taking a horseback ride that takes about an hour. Once you reach the waterfall, you can admire the beauty and power of the water, or swim in the natural pool at the base. You can also visit the nearby butterfly garden, where you can see colorful butterflies and flowers. This attraction is suitable for children of 6 years and older, and it will give you a refreshing and relaxing experience.

## *Child-Friendly Accommodation*

Below are some of the best child-friendly accommodation in Costa Rica:

**Tamarindo Diria**: This is a beachfront resort located in the lively town of Tamarindo, on the Pacific coast. The resort has spacious rooms and suites that can accommodate up to six people, and some of them have balconies or terraces with ocean views. The resort also has four pools, including a kids pool and a pool with a slide, as well as a playground, a game room, and a kids club. The resort offers a buffet breakfast, and has several restaurants and bars that serve a variety of cuisines. The resort is also close to the magnificent Playa Tamarindo, where you can enjoy surfing, kayaking, or snorkeling, or join a boat tour to see dolphins and whales.

**Rafiki Safari Lodge**: This is an eco-friendly lodge located in the rainforest, near the Savegre River. The lodge has safari-style tents that can sleep up to four people, and have private bathrooms, hot water, and electricity. The lodge also has a pool, a restaurant, and a bar, and offers free Wi-Fi in the common areas. The lodge offers a range of activities for families, such as rafting, hiking, horseback riding, birdwatching, and wildlife tours. You can also visit the nearby Quetzal National Park, where you can see the rare and beautiful quetzal bird.

**Peace Lodge and Waterfall Gardens**: This is a luxury lodge located in the cloud forest, near the Poas Volcano. The lodge has elegant rooms and suites that can sleep up to five people, and have fireplaces, jacuzzis, and balconies with hammocks. The lodge also has a pool, a spa, a restaurant, and a bar, and offers free Wi-Fi and breakfast. The lodge is part of the La Paz Waterfall

Gardens, where you can see stunning waterfalls, butterflies, hummingbirds, and orchids. You can also visit the animal sanctuary, where you can see jaguars, monkeys, sloths, and toucans.

**Arenal Manoa:** This is a family-friendly hotel located in the Arenal Volcano area. The hotel has cozy rooms and suites that can sleep up to four people, and have private gardens and terraces with volcano views. The hotel also has two pools, one of them with a kids section, a spa, a restaurant, and a bar, and offers free Wi-Fi and breakfast. The hotel offers a shuttle service to the nearby hot springs, where you can relax in the natural thermal waters. You can also enjoy some of the adventure activities in the area, such as zip-lining, rafting, or hiking.

**Karahé Beach Hotel**: This is a beachfront hotel located in the Manuel Antonio area, on the Pacific coast. The hotel has comfortable rooms and villas that can sleep up to six people, and have air conditioning, cable TV, and mini-fridges. The hotel also has a pool, a restaurant, and a bar, and offers free Wi-Fi and breakfast. The hotel is close to the beautiful Playa Espadilla, where you can swim, sunbathe, or play in the sand. You can also visit the Manuel Antonio National

Park, where you can see a variety of animals, such as monkeys, sloths, iguanas, and birds.

# Chapter 13 • Travelling on a Budget

## *Budget-Friendly Accommodation*

Below are some of the best budget-friendly accommodation in Costa Rica:

**Hostels**: Some of the best hostels in Costa Rica are Pagalù Hostel in Puerto Viejo, Hostel Cattleya in Monteverde, and Selina Hostel in San Jose.

**Cabins**: Cabins are usually wooden structures that offer basic amenities, such as beds, bathrooms, and electricity. Some cabins also have kitchens, balconies, or hammocks. Cabins are usually located in rural or natural areas, such as forests, mountains, or beaches. Some of the best cabins in Costa Rica are Cabinas Jimenez in Puerto Jimenez, Cabinas El Pueblo in Santa Elena, and Cabinas Las Olas in Playa Avellanas.

**Hotels**: Some of the best hotels in Costa Rica are Hotel 1915 INN & SUITES in Alajuela, Arenal Xilopalo in La Fortuna, and Karahé Beach Hotel in Manuel Antonio.

## *Cheap Eats and Local Food*

Below are some of the best cheap eats and local food in Costa Rica:

**Gallo Pinto**: This is the most typical and popular breakfast dish in Costa Rica, and it consists of white rice and black or red beans, sautéed with onions, peppers, and cilantro. It is usually served with eggs, cheese, tortillas, plantains, and sour cream. Gallo Pinto is a hearty and nutritious meal that will give you energy for the day. You can find it in almost any restaurant or soda (local diner) for around $4-$7 per person.

**Casado**: This is the most common and filling lunch or dinner dish in Costa Rica, and it consists of a plate with rice, beans, salad, fried plantains, and a choice of meat, fish, or chicken. Casado means "married" in Spanish, and it refers to the combination of different ingredients that make a balanced and complete meal. Casado is a great way to try the local cuisine and enjoy a variety of flavors. You can find it in most sodas for around $5-$10 per person.

**Sopa Negra**: This is a traditional soup that is made with black beans, onions, garlic, cilantro, and eggs. It is a rich and flavorful soup that is often eaten as a starter or a main course. Sopa Negra is a comfort food that is perfect for cold or rainy days. You can find it in some sodas or restaurants for around $3-$6 per person.

**Ceviche**: This is a fresh and light dish that is made with raw fish or seafood, marinated in lime juice, onions, peppers, cilantro, and salt. It is a refreshing and tangy dish that is often eaten as a snack or an appetizer. Ceviche is a popular dish in coastal areas, where you can find the freshest and best quality fish and seafood. You can find it in some sodas, restaurants, or street stalls for around $4-$8 per person.

**Chifrijo**: This is a tasty and satisfying snack that is made with rice, beans, fried pork, pico de gallo (tomato and onion salsa), and avocado. It is served in a bowl with tortilla chips or bread. Chifrijo is a crunchy and creamy dish that is ideal for sharing with friends or family. You can find it in some bars, sodas, or restaurants for around $3-$5 per person.

## *Free and Affordable Attractions*

There are many free and affordable attractions that you can visit and experience in Costa Rica. Below are some of the best ones:

**National Parks**: Costa Rica has more than 20 national

parks that cover about 25% of the country's territory. These parks protect some of the most diverse and unique ecosystems in the world, and are home to a wide range of animals and plants. You can visit these parks and enjoy hiking, birdwatching, wildlife viewing, and scenic views. The entrance fees vary for each park, but they are generally low, ranging from free to $20 USD per person. Some of the most popular and beautiful national parks in Costa Rica are Cahuita National Park, which is free and has a stunning coral reef and beach; Manuel Antonio National Park, which costs $16 USD and has a variety of monkeys, sloths, and birds; and Poas Volcano National Park, which costs $15 USD and has an impressive crater and lake.

**Waterfalls**: Costa Rica has many waterfalls that are hidden in the rainforest, mountains, or valleys. These waterfalls are a great attraction for nature lovers, as they offer refreshing and relaxing experiences. You can admire the beauty and power of the water, swim in the natural pools, or picnic in the surroundings. Some of the waterfalls are free to visit, while others charge a small fee or require a guide. Some of the best waterfalls in Costa Rica are La Fortuna Waterfall, which costs $18 USD and is near the Arenal Volcano; Montezuma Falls, which is free and has three cascades and a rope swing5; and Nauyaca Waterfalls, which costs $8 USD and has two spectacular falls and a large pool.

**Beaches**: Costa Rica has more than 800 miles of coastline, with beaches on both the Pacific and Caribbean sides. These beaches are some of the most beautiful and diverse in the world, and offer a variety of activities and attractions. You can swim, sunbathe, surf, snorkel, kayak, or just relax on the sand. Most of the beaches are free to access, while some may charge a small fee or require a park entrance. Some of the best beaches in Costa Rica are Playa Conchal, which is free and has white sand made of crushed shells; Playa Tamarindo, which is free and has a lively town and great surfing; and Playa Tortuga, which is free and has a turtle nesting and hatching site.

**Museums**: Costa Rica has many museums that showcase the history, culture, and art of the country. These museums are a great attraction for culture and education seekers, as they offer interesting and informative exhibits and displays. Some of the museums are free to visit, while others charge a low fee or have a donation system. Some of the best museums in Costa Rica are the National Museum, which is free and has exhibits of pre-Columbian art, colonial history, and natural history; the Gold Museum, which costs $11 USD and has a collection of gold artifacts from different indigenous cultures; and the Jade Museum, which costs $15 USD and has a collection of jade objects and sculptures.

## *Transportation Tips for Saving Money*

Costa Rica offers many attractions and activities for travelers who want to enjoy its natural beauty, wildlife, culture, and adventure. However, getting around the country can be a challenge, especially if you are traveling on a budget. Fortunately, there are some tips and options that can help you save money on transportation in Costa Rica. Below are some of them:

**Take the public bus**. The public bus is the cheapest and most common way to travel around Costa Rica. The buses are usually reliable, comfortable, and safe, and they cover most of the country's destinations. You can find the bus schedules, routes, and fares on the official website of the Costa Rican Transportation Council. You can buy the bus tickets at the bus stations, kiosks, or online, depending on the bus company. The bus fares vary depending on the distance and the service, but they are generally low, ranging from $1 to $20 USD per person. For example, a bus ride from San Jose to La Fortuna costs around $5 USD, and a bus ride from San Jose to Manuel Antonio costs around $10 USD.

**Rent a car.** Renting a car can be a convenient and flexible way to explore Costa Rica, especially if you want to visit off-the-beaten-path locations or have your own schedule. However, renting a car can also be expensive, due to the high insurance and taxes. To save money on renting a car, you can follow these tips:

**Book in advance and compare prices.** You can find the best deals and discounts on car rentals by booking online and comparing prices from different car rental companies. Some of the most popular and reliable car rental companies in Costa Rica are Adobe, Alamo, Budget, Enterprise, and Vamos.

**Decline the insurance that is allowed.** The car rental companies in Costa Rica will offer you various types of insurance, such as liability, collision, theft, and personal. However, some of these insurance are optional, and you can decline them if you have your own insurance or credit card coverage. The only mandatory insurance in Costa Rica is the basic liability insurance, which costs around $10 to $20 USD per day.

**Use a GPS or offline maps.** Driving in Costa Rica can be challenging, due to the poor road conditions, lack of signs, and heavy traffic. To avoid getting lost or wasting time and gas, it is advisable to use a GPS or offline maps, such as Google Maps or Waze, to navigate and plan your routes. You can rent a GPS from the car rental company, or use your own smartphone or device. However, renting a GPS can cost around $10 USD per day, so it may be cheaper to use your own device and buy a local SIM card with data, which costs around $2 to $5 USD.

**Use shared shuttles or private transfers.** If you don't want to take the public bus or rent a car, you can also use shared shuttles or private transfers to get around Costa Rica. These are comfortable and convenient options that will pick you up and drop you off at your desired locations, without having to worry about driving, parking, or schedules. However, these options are also more expensive than the public bus, and they may not be available for all destinations. To save money on shared shuttles or private transfers, you can follow these tips:

**Book online and in advance.** You can find the best deals and discounts on shared shuttles or private transfers by booking online and in advance. You can use online platforms, such as Interbus, Gray Line, or Caribe Shuttle.

**Travel in groups or with other travelers**. You can save money on shared shuttles or private transfers by traveling in groups or with other travelers. The more people you travel with, the lower the price per person will be. You can also join or create groups with other travelers who are going to the same destination, and split the cost of the transportation.

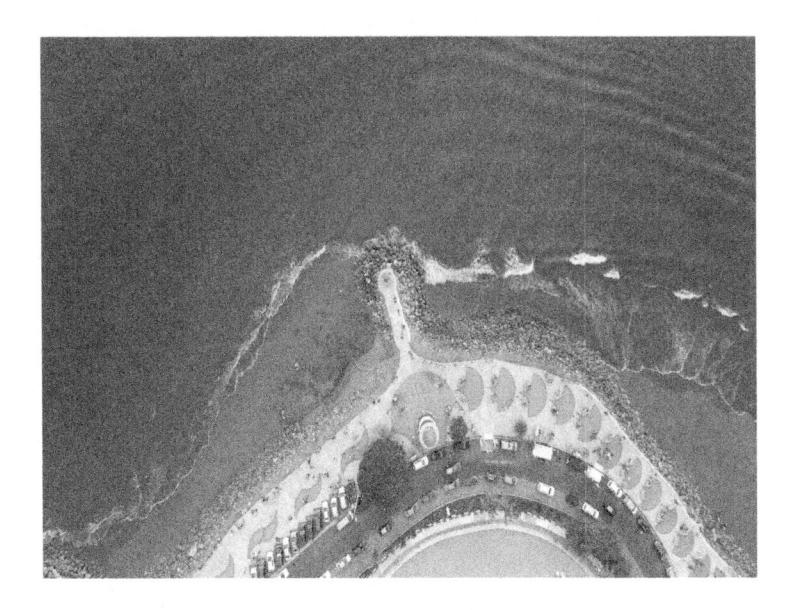

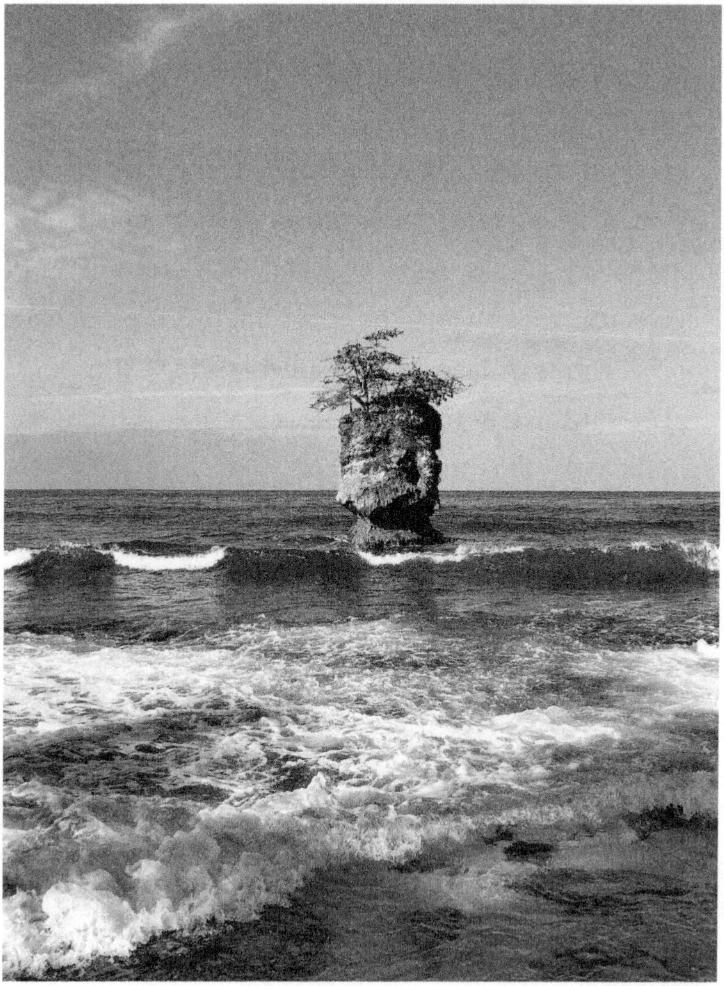

# Chapter 14 • Day Trips and Excursions

## *Panama City*

Panama City is the capital and largest city of Panama, a country that borders Costa Rica to the south. Panama City is a diverse and multicultural city that offers a lot of attractions and activities for travelers who want to enjoy its natural beauty, wildlife, culture, and adventure. Below are some of the highlights of Panama City:

**The Panama Canal:** This is the most famous and impressive attraction in Panama City, and it is a must-see for any visitor. The Panama Canal is a man-made waterway that connects the Atlantic and Pacific oceans, and allows ships to pass through without having to go around South America. The canal is considered one of the engineering marvels of the world, and it has a significant economic and historical impact. You can visit the Miraflores Visitor Center, where you can see the canal in action, watch a documentary, and learn about its history and operation. You can also take a boat tour or a train ride along the canal, and experience the amazing views and scenery.

**Casco Viejo**: This is the historic and cultural center of Panama City, and it is a UNESCO World Heritage Site. Casco Viejo, also known as the Old City, is a charming and colorful neighborhood that dates back to the 17th century. It was the second settlement of Panama City, after the original one was destroyed by a pirate attack. You can walk along the cobblestone streets and admire the colonial architecture, churches, plazas, and monuments. You can also visit some of the museums, such as the Panama Canal Museum, the National Theater, or the Gold Museum, and learn about the history and culture of Panama. You can also enjoy some of the nightlife and entertainment options, such as bars, restaurants, and live music.

**Amador Causeway**: This is a scenic and recreational area that connects four islands in the Pacific Ocean. The causeway was built with the rocks that were excavated from the Panama Canal, and it offers stunning views of the city skyline and the canal. You can walk, bike, or rollerblade along the causeway, and enjoy the breeze and the nature. You can also visit some of the attractions, such as the Biomuseo, a museum designed by the famous architect Frank Gehry, that showcases the biodiversity and history of Panama. You can also visit the Punta Culebra Nature Center, where you can see marine life, such as turtles, sharks, and rays. You can also enjoy some of the water sports and activities, such as kayaking, sailing, or fishing.

**Avenida Balboa:** This is the main avenue and waterfront of Panama City, and it is a modern and vibrant area that contrasts with the old city. Avenida Balboa is lined with skyscrapers, hotels, and shopping malls, and it offers a variety of services and amenities. You can walk along the Cinta Costera, a pedestrian and bike path that runs along the coast, and enjoy the views and the atmosphere. You can also visit some of the attractions, such as the Multicentro, a shopping mall that has a casino, a cinema, and a Hard Rock Cafe. You can also visit the F&F Tower, a twisted tower that is one of the landmarks of the city. You can also enjoy some of the nightlife and entertainment options, such as clubs, bars, and restaurants.

## *Granada*

If you are interested in visiting Granada, you can find some information and tips below.

Granada is the oldest colonial city in Nicaragua, and one of the most beautiful and charming in Central America.

It is located on the shores of Lake Nicaragua, and it has a rich history and culture that reflects its Spanish, Moorish, and indigenous influences. Granada is also a great base for exploring the natural attractions and activities around the lake, such as volcanoes, islands, and wildlife.

Some of the best things to do and see in Granada are:

**Visit the Cathedral of Granada**, a stunning yellow and white building that dominates the central plaza. The cathedral was built in the 16th century, and it has a neoclassical style with baroque details. You can admire the facade, the interior, and the bell tower, and enjoy the views of the city and the lake. The entrance fee is $1 USD per person.

**Explore the historic center of Granada**, where you can see the colonial architecture, churches, plazas, and monuments. You can walk along the colorful streets and admire the old houses and buildings, some of which have been converted into museums, hotels, or restaurants. You can also visit some of the museums, such as the Casa de los Leones, which showcases the history and culture of Granada, or the ChocoMuseo, which offers chocolate workshops and tastings.

**Take a boat tour of the Islets of Granada**, a group

of more than 300 small islands that are scattered in Lake Nicaragua. The islands are home to a variety of wildlife, such as birds, monkeys, and turtles, and some of them have restaurants, hotels, or private residences. You can take a boat tour from the port of Granada, and enjoy the scenery and the nature. The boat tour costs around $15 USD per person, and it lasts about two hours.

**Visit the Mombacho Volcano Natural Reserve**, a protected area that covers the slopes and the crater of the Mombacho Volcano. The volcano is dormant, but it offers stunning views of the lake and the city. You can hike along the trails that lead to the crater, where you can see the cloud forest, the fumaroles, and the orchids. You can also zip-line through the canopy, and experience the thrill and the beauty of the forest. The entrance fee to the reserve is $5 USD per person, and the zip-line costs around $30 USD per person.

**Enjoy the nightlife and the cuisine of Granada**, where you can find a variety of bars, restaurants, and cafes that cater to different tastes and budgets. You can try some of the local specialties, such as vigorón, a dish of boiled yuca, pork rinds, and cabbage salad, or gallo pinto, a dish of rice and beans. You can also taste some of the international cuisines, such as Italian, French, or Mexican. You can also enjoy some of the live music, dancing, and entertainment that Granada offers, especially on the weekends.

## *Bocas del Toro*

If you are interested in visiting Bocas del Toro, below is some information and tips that you may find useful.

Bocas del Toro is located on the Caribbean Sea, near the border with Costa Rica. It has a diverse and multicultural population, influenced by Spanish, African, indigenous, and Caribbean cultures. It is also known for its natural beauty, wildlife, culture, and adventure. You can enjoy activities such as scuba diving, snorkeling, sailing, surfing, hiking, and wildlife watching. You can also explore the colonial architecture, museums, and nightlife of Bocas Town, the capital and main tourist hub of the province.

**To get to Bocas del Toro**, you have several options. You can fly from Panama City or San Jose, Costa Rica, to Bocas Town, which takes about an hour and costs around $100-$200 USD per person. You can also take a bus from Panama City or San Jose to Almirante, the port town on the mainland, which takes about 10-12 hours and costs around $30-$40 USD per person. From Almirante, you can take a boat to Bocas Town, which takes about 30 minutes and costs around $6 USD per person. You can also rent a car and drive to Almirante, which takes about 8-10 hours and costs around $50-$100 USD per day.

**To get around Bocas del Toro,** you have several options. You can take a water taxi, which is the most common and convenient way to travel between the islands. The water taxis are usually available at the docks or by phone, and they charge around $1-$10 USD per person, depending on the distance and the number of passengers. You can also rent a bike, which is a cheap and eco-friendly way to explore the islands. The bike rentals are usually available at the hotels or shops, and they charge around $5-$10 USD per day. You can also rent a scooter, which is a fast and fun way to explore the islands. The scooter rentals are usually available at the hotels or shops, and they charge around $20-$30 USD per day.

**To stay in Bocas del Toro**, you have several options. You can choose from a variety of accommodation types, such as hotels, hostels, cabins, villas, or resorts. The prices vary depending on the location, quality, and season, but they are generally affordable and competitive. Some of the recommended accommodation options are: Red Frog Beach Island Resort, Hotel Bocas del Toro, Popa Paradise Beach Resort.

**To eat in Bocas del Toro**, you have several options. You can try some of the local specialties, such as patacones, fried plantain slices; ceviche, raw fish or seafood marinated in lime juice; or chifrijo, a bowl of rice, beans, fried pork, salsa, and avocado. You can also taste some of the international cuisines, such as Italian, French, or Mexican. Some of the recommended restaurants and bars are: Leaf Eaters Cafe, The Blue Coconut, The Firefly Restaurant & Bar.

These are some of the information and tips that you may find useful for visiting Bocas del Toro. However, there are many more things to do and see in this beautiful and diverse province of Panama. Whatever you decide to do, you will surely have a wonderful and unforgettable time in Bocas del Toro.

## *San Juan del Sur*

If you are interested in visiting San Juan del Sur, below is some information that you may find useful.

San Juan del Sur is located on the Pacific Ocean, in the

Rivas department, about 140 kilometers south of Managua, the capital of Nicaragua. It is a popular destination for surfers, beach lovers, and nature enthusiasts. It has a population of about 15,500 people, who are mostly engaged in fishing, tourism, or food and beverage industries. It also has a diverse and multicultural community, influenced by Spanish, African, indigenous, and Caribbean cultures.

Some of the main attractions and activities in San Juan del Sur are:

**The beach and the bay**: San Juan del Sur has a crescent-shaped bay that offers a stunning view of the ocean and the town. The beach is a great place to relax, swim, sunbathe, or play in the sand. You can also enjoy some of the water sports and activities, such as surfing, kayaking, snorkeling, or sailing. You can also join a boat tour to see dolphins, whales, or turtles. The beach is also close to the main services and amenities of the town, such as restaurants, bars, shops, and hotels.

**The Christ of the Mercy**: This is a 25-meter statue of Jesus that overlooks the town from a hill on the northern end of the bay. It is one of the tallest statues of Jesus in the world, and it offers a panoramic view of the town and the ocean. You can hike up to the statue, which takes about an hour, or take a taxi or a shuttle. The entrance fee is $2 USD per person.

**The petroglyph**: This is a spectacular rock carving that depicts a hunting scene, dating back to about 1500 years ago. It is located near the town, and you can walk to it, which takes about 20 minutes, or take a taxi or a shuttle. The petroglyph is a cultural and historical treasure that shows the ancient art and life of the indigenous people of the region.

**The Casa de Cultura**: This is a cultural center that offers salsa, merengue, and bachata dance lessons, art exhibits, and more. It is also the home of the APC (Association of Cultural Promoters), a local organization that promotes the arts and culture of San Juan del Sur. You can visit the Casa de Cultura and learn about the local traditions and talents, or join some of the events and workshops that they organize.

## *Ometepe Island*

If you are interested in visiting Ometepe Island, below is some information that you may find useful.

Ometepe Island is the largest island in Lake Nicaragua, the largest lake in Central America. It is formed by two volcanoes, Concepción and Maderas, that are connected by a narrow isthmus. The island has a rich history, culture, and biodiversity, and it is a UNESCO Biosphere Reserve.

Some of the main attractions and activities on Ometepe Island are:

**Hiking the volcanoes**: You can hike to the summit of either Concepción or Maderas, or both, depending on your fitness level and time. Concepción is an active volcano that offers stunning views of the lake and the island, but it is also more challenging and requires a guide. Maderas is a dormant volcano that has a cloud forest and a crater lake, but it is also more muddy and slippery. Both hikes take about 8 to 10 hours round trip, and cost around $25 to $35 USD per person, including the guide and the entrance fee.

**Visiting the petroglyphs and stone idols**: You can see the ancient rock carvings and sculptures that date back to pre-Columbian times, and learn about the history and culture of the indigenous people of the island. There are more than 1700 petroglyphs and 300 stone idols scattered around the island, but some of the most accessible and impressive ones are located near the villages of Altagracia and Balgüe. You can visit them on your own or with a guide, and the entrance fee is around

$2 USD per person.

**Swimming in the natural pools**: You can cool off and relax in the natural pools that are formed by the rivers and waterfalls on the island. Some of the most popular ones are Ojo de Agua, a spring-fed pool with clear and refreshing water; San Ramón Waterfall, a 50-meter cascade that plunges into a rocky pool; and Charco Verde, a lagoon surrounded by a nature reserve. You can access them by walking, biking, or taking a taxi, and the entrance fee is around $3 to $5 USD per person.

**Exploring the Islets of Granada**: You can take a boat tour to the Islets of Granada, a group of more than 300 small islands that are located in Lake Nicaragua, near the city of Granada. The islands are home to a variety of wildlife, such as birds, monkeys, and turtles, and some of them have restaurants, hotels, or private residences. You can take a boat tour from the port of Granada, and enjoy the scenery and the nature. The boat tour costs around $15 USD per person, and it lasts about two hours.

# Chapter 15 • Sustainability and Responsible Travel

## *Sustainable Tourism in Costa Rica*

Costa Rica is a country that has been a pioneer and a leader in sustainable tourism, which is a form of tourism that respects and protects the environment, the culture, and the well-being of the local communities. Some of the aspects that make Costa Rica a sustainable tourism destination are:

**Renewable energy:** Costa Rica produces more than 98% of its electricity from renewable sources, such as hydro, wind, geothermal, solar, and biomass. This reduces the greenhouse gas emissions and the dependence on fossil fuels. Costa Rica also promotes the use of electric vehicles and public transportation, and has plans to electrify 70% of its buses and taxis by 2035.

**Protected areas**: Costa Rica has more than 25% of its territory designated as protected areas, such as national parks, wildlife reserves, and biosphere reserves. These areas conserve the biodiversity and the ecosystems of the country, which are among the richest and most diverse in the world. Costa Rica has more than 6% of the global biodiversity, and hosts more than 900 species of birds, 200 species of mammals, 400 species of reptiles and amphibians, and 10,000 species of plants. The protected areas also offer a variety of attractions and activities for tourists, such as hiking, birdwatching, wildlife viewing, and scenic views.

**Ecotourism**: Costa Rica has developed a model of ecotourism that involves the participation and empowerment of the local communities, the respect and appreciation of the culture and the traditions, and the education and awareness of the environmental and social issues. Costa Rica has a certification program for sustainable tourism (CST), which evaluates and recognizes the tourism businesses that comply with the standards of sustainability in terms of management, social, environmental, and economic aspects. Costa Rica also has a network of rural community tourism (ACTUAR), which offers authentic and responsible experiences for tourists, such as homestays, cultural activities, gastronomy, and handicrafts.

These are some of the aspects that make Costa Rica a sustainable tourism destination, but there are many more to discover and enjoy, depending on your preferences and interests. Costa Rica is a country that invites you to experience its natural beauty, wildlife, culture, and adventure, while also contributing to its conservation and development.

## *Eco-Friendly Accommodation and Transportation*

If you are looking for eco-friendly accommodation and transportation in Costa Rica, below are some tips and suggestions that you may find useful:

**Eco-friendly accommodation**: Costa Rica has a wide range of accommodation types that are eco-friendly, such as eco-lodges, cabins, villas, or resorts. These accommodation options are designed to minimize their impact on the environment, and to support the local communities and culture. Some of the features that make them eco-friendly are:

They use renewable energy sources, such as solar, wind, or hydro power, to generate electricity and hot water.

They have water conservation and recycling systems, such as rainwater harvesting, greywater reuse, or composting toilets.

They use organic and biodegradable products, such as

soap, shampoo, or cleaning products, and avoid single-use plastic items, such as bottles, straws, or bags.

They have organic and local food options, such as fruits, vegetables, or coffee, and avoid imported or processed food items.

They have activities and programs that educate and involve the guests in the environmental and social issues, such as wildlife tours, cultural workshops, or volunteer opportunities.

Some of the best eco-friendly accommodation options in Costa Rica are:

**Lapa Rios Lodge**: This is a luxury eco-lodge located in the Osa Peninsula, one of the most biodiverse places on earth. The lodge has 17 bungalows that are built with natural materials and have open-air design, offering stunning views of the rainforest and the ocean. The lodge also has a pool, a spa, a restaurant, and a bar, and offers free Wi-Fi and breakfast. The lodge offers a range of activities for guests, such as hiking, birdwatching, wildlife viewing, and surfing. The lodge is also part of the National Geographic Unique Lodges of the World, and has a certification for sustainable tourism (CST) of five leaves, the highest level possible.

**Finca Luna Nueva Lodge**: This is a cozy and

affordable eco-lodge located in the Arenal Volcano area. The lodge has 14 rooms and cabins that are built with organic and recycled materials and have private bathrooms and balconies. The lodge also has a pool, a spa, a restaurant, and a bar, and offers free Wi-Fi and breakfast. The lodge is located on a 200-acre organic farm, where guests can see and taste various crops, such as cacao, ginger, or turmeric. The lodge also offers a range of activities for guests, such as yoga, meditation, cooking classes, and hot springs. The lodge has a CST of four leaves.

**Selva Bananito Lodge:** This is a rustic and charming eco-lodge located in the Caribbean coast, near the border with Panama. The lodge has 11 cabins that are built with wood and have private bathrooms and hammocks. The lodge also has a restaurant and a bar, and offers free breakfast and dinner. The lodge is located on a 2,000-acre private reserve, where guests can see and hear various animals, such as monkeys, sloths, and toucans. The lodge also offers a range of activities for guests, such as zip-lining, horseback riding, rafting, and hiking. The lodge has a CST of five leaves.

**Eco-friendly transportation**: Costa Rica has various transportation options that are eco-friendly, such as public buses, shared shuttles, electric vehicles, or bikes. These transportation options are designed to reduce the greenhouse gas emissions and the dependence on fossil fuels. Some of the features that make them eco-friendly are:

They use renewable energy sources, such as hydro or solar power, to charge their batteries or fuel their engines.

They have low emission and high efficiency standards, such as Euro 6 or hybrid technology, to optimize their performance and reduce their pollution.

They have smart and integrated systems, such as GPS or online platforms, to plan and coordinate their routes and schedules.

They have incentives and benefits, such as discounts or priority lanes, to encourage their use and adoption.

Some of the best eco-friendly transportation options in Costa Rica are:

**Public buses**: This is the cheapest and most common way to travel around Costa Rica. The buses are usually reliable, comfortable, and safe, and they cover most of the country's destinations. You can buy the bus tickets at the bus stations, kiosks, or online, depending on the bus company. The bus fares vary depending on the distance and the service, but they are generally low, ranging from $1 to $20 USD per person. For example, a bus ride from San Jose to La Fortuna costs around $5 USD, and a bus ride from San Jose to Manuel Antonio costs around $10 USD.

**Shared shuttles**: This is a comfortable and convenient way to travel around Costa Rica, especially if you want to visit off-the-beaten-path locations or have your own schedule. Shared shuttles are vans or minibuses that pick you up and drop you off at your desired locations, without having to worry about driving, parking, or schedules. Some of the most popular and reliable shuttle companies in Costa Rica are Interbus, Gray Line, and Caribe Shuttle. The shuttle fares vary depending on the distance and the service, but they are generally affordable and competitive, ranging from $10 to $50 USD per person. For example, a shuttle ride from San Jose to Monteverde costs around $30 USD, and a shuttle ride from San Jose to Puerto Viejo costs around $40 USD.

**Electric vehicles**: This is a modern and eco-friendly way to explore Costa Rica, especially if you want to have more flexibility and autonomy. Electric vehicles are cars or motorcycles that run on electricity, and have zero

emissions and low noise. Some of the most popular and reliable rental companies in Costa Rica are Adobe, Alamo, and Vamos. The rental fares vary depending on the type and the duration of the vehicle, but they are generally reasonable and competitive, ranging from $20 to $100 USD per day. For example, an electric car rental for a week costs around $300 USD, and an electric motorcycle rental for a week costs around $200 USD.
**Bikes**: This is a cheap and eco-friendly way to explore Costa Rica, especially if you want to enjoy the nature and the scenery. Bikes are pedal-powered vehicles that have zero emissions and low impact. Some of the most popular and reliable bike rental companies in Costa Rica are Bike Arenal, Bike Station CR, and Bike Rental Costa Rica. The bike rental fares vary depending on the type and the duration of the bike, but they are generally low and affordable, ranging from $5 to $10 USD per day. For example, a mountain bike rental for a day costs around $8 USD, and a road bike rental for a day costs around $10 USD.

## *Ethical Experiences and Wildlife Conservation*

If you are looking for ethical experiences and wildlife

conservation in Costa Rica, below are some tips and suggestions that you may find useful:

**Choose eco-friendly accommodation and transportation options.** Costa Rica has a wide range of accommodation and transportation options that are eco-friendly, such as eco-lodges, cabins, villas, or resorts, and public buses, shared shuttles, electric vehicles, or bikes. These options are designed to minimize their impact on the environment, and to support the local communities and culture.

**Participate in ecotourism and wildlife conservation programs.** Costa Rica has many ecotourism and wildlife conservation programs that offer authentic and responsible experiences for tourists, such as wildlife tours, cultural workshops, volunteer opportunities, or research projects. These programs involve the participation and empowerment of the local communities, the respect and appreciation of the culture and the traditions, and the education and awareness of the environmental and social issues.

**Follow the guidelines and best practices for ethical wildlife watching.** Costa Rica has a rich and diverse wildlife, and watching it can be an incredible experience. However, it is important to do so responsibly, and to avoid harming or disturbing the animals or their habitats. Some of the guidelines and best practices for ethical wildlife watching are:

Always follow the instructions of local authorities and conservation organizations. They are designed to protect both wildlife and visitors.

Keep a safe and respectful distance from the animals, and do not touch, feed, or chase them. Use binoculars, cameras, or telephoto lenses to observe them.

Do not use flash, artificial lights, or loud noises when watching the animals, as they can stress or scare them. Turn off your phone, radio, or music player, and speak softly.

Do not litter, damage, or collect any natural or cultural objects, such as plants, rocks, shells, or artifacts. Leave no trace of your visit, and take only memories and photos.

Support the local conservation efforts and initiatives, such as donating, volunteering, or buying souvenirs from local artisans or organizations.

# Conclusion

Costa Rica is a country that has something for everyone, whether you are looking for nature, wildlife, culture, or adventure. It is a country that is committed to sustainability and environmental protection, and that offers a variety of eco-friendly and ethical experiences. It is also a country that has a diverse and multicultural population, that welcomes and respects visitors from all over the world.

In this travel guide, we have covered some of the best attractions, activities, accommodation, transportation, and tips that Costa Rica has to offer. However, there is much more to discover and enjoy in this beautiful and amazing country. We hope that this travel guide has inspired you to visit Costa Rica, and that you will have a memorable and enjoyable time there. Thank you for choosing our travel guide, and we wish you a happy and safe journey. Pura vida!

Printed in Great Britain
by Amazon